THE Kitchen Envy COOKBOOK

Milk

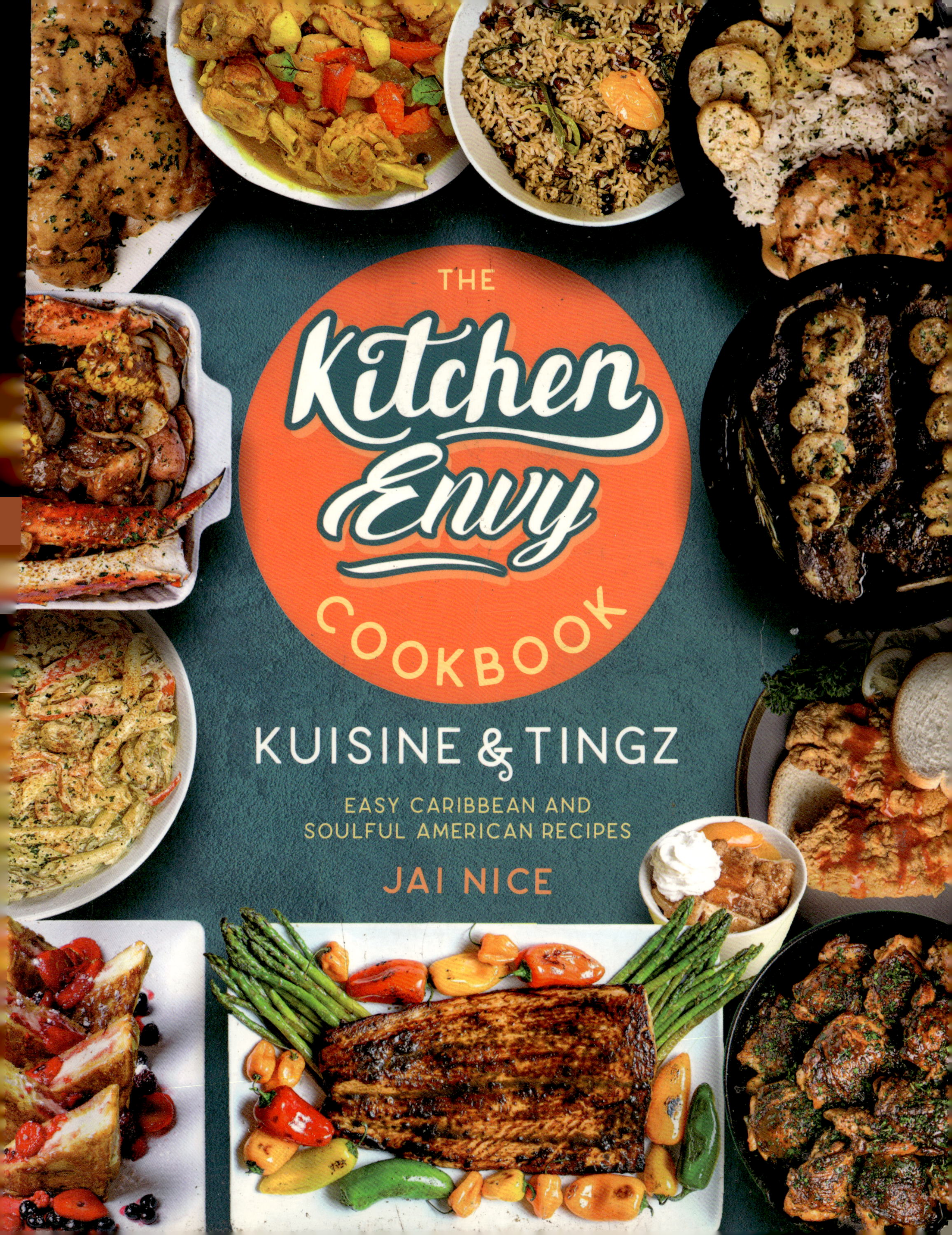
THE
Kitchen Envy
COOKBOOK
KUISINE & TINGZ
EASY CARIBBEAN AND
SOULFUL AMERICAN RECIPES
JAI NICE

THE Kitchen Envy COOKBOOK

KUISINE & TINGZ

JAI NICE

EASY CARIBBEAN AND
SOULFUL AMERICAN RECIPES

The recipes within this book were created for the ingredients and techniques indicated. Individual results may vary due to inconsistencies in elements such as ingredients, cooking temperatures, typos, errors, omissions, or individual cooking ability. The author and publisher of this book are not responsible for any allergies or adverse reactions that you may have to the recipes in this book, whether the recipe has been expressly followed or modified.

LCCN: 2020918557
ISBN-13: 978-0-578-77123-6

Author: Jai Nice

Book Design: The Book Designers

Printed in China

CONTENTS

INTRO

Whenever someone asks what my passion is, I say fashion is my first love, but cooking is where my heart is. I love cooking for the same reason that I love fashion – the thrill of creating something new. Like designing clothes, I can take what's in my head and bring the vision to life. In the kitchen, making a new recipe that tastes amazing is therapeutic for me.

I developed a love and passion for cooking in my Grandmother's kitchen. Helping her cook meals for the family was how we bonded and spent quality time. I grew up in a full house, so large meals came out of my Granny's kitchen daily. And I still love to cook meals for my family and friends, to this day. My house is the go to for holidays, get-togethers, and game nights. I'm always in the kitchen whipping up a feast for everyone to enjoy. Funny enough, it's not eating the meal that I enjoy most. My pleasure comes from giving. I love to cook for others and see the satisfaction on their faces when they take a bite of my food. It feels like I'm back to the days of cooking in my Grandmother's kitchen.

Granny taught me many things in that kitchen; like how to make homemade pound cake ...RIGHT! When I was younger, I helped my Granny bake her famous pound cake – known for being moist, rich, and delicious. It was the first time I had baked a cake, so I didn't know how important it was to sift and measure the flour before mixing it into the batter. When the cake came out chewy, like bubble gum, my Granny had me bake it all over again! I remember that day vividly because it was the first time I realized the importance of perfecting a recipe so the dish comes out amazing.

The kitchen is a place to experience happy vibes, make great memories and bond with loved ones. I felt that back in my Granny's kitchen, and I feel it now in my own kitchen with my daughter. My grandmother's style of teaching is "watch and learn." With my daughter, I am more hands on. She actually helps me cook and deserves so much credit for this book since her input goes into almost everything I make. She loves when I try new things in the kitchen, so I decided to cook and create different recipes daily. When I started my cooking page on Instagram, she was my videographer and creative director! She recorded my cooking tutorials and helped me edit them. In April 2020, we posted a few cooking tutorials that people fell in love with. The overwhelming response inspired me to keep cooking.

A substantial part of my cooking style is derived from my Jamaican heritage. My upbringing was blended with African American and Caribbean culture. Learning the cornerstones of these rich cuisines was crucial to my development in the kitchen and in life. You'll find that blend reflected in this cookbook with recipes like my jerk chicken tacos! There's also soul food favorites, low calorie meals, vegan vibes, and many other things to try. I hope you enjoy these recipes as much as I do and that you share them with those you love.

Before we begin, I must emphasize how thankful I am for my supporters. Their constant encouragement pushed me to create this cookbook for them. I hope all of you, especially those with little experience in the kitchen, understand that anyone can cook – it just takes time and the proper instructions. Not everyone grew up in a house that cultivated a knowledge of cooking, and that is nothing to be ashamed of. I am certain that you will learn the basics of cooking, and realize that home-cooked meals can be easy, fun, and very rewarding.

Let's get cooking!

MY PLEASURE COMES FROM GIVING. I LOVE TO COOK FOR OTHERS AND SEE THE SATISFACTION ON THEIR FACES WHEN THEY TAKE A BITE OF MY FOOD.

KITCHEN ESSENTIALS

Welcome to the Kitchen Envy Cookbook: Kuisine and Tingz! I am confident that you'll have a blast whipping up my favorite recipes!

I have prepared a checklist of "must-have" items for creating the recipes in this book. Cooking is so much easier (and faster) when you have the proper tools to get the job done!

If you don't know where to find these items, check out my Kitchen Envy line of exclusive cookware and utensils at www.thekitchenenvy.com

Cleaning and Sanitization

- Water
- White vinegar
- The Cleaning Method: Use water and vinegar to rinse the meats, especially chicken and seafood. With vinegar, a little bit goes a long way!

The Must-Haves

- All-Purpose Flour
- Butter (salted or unsalted)
- Eggs
- Milk (preferably whole)
- Olive Oil (Extra Virgin)
- Vegetable Oil (Always use enough oil to completely submerge the food when you are frying.)
- White Sugar

Seasonings

- Beef Stock
- Bell Peppers
- Black Pepper
- Blackened Seasoning
- Cayenne Pepper
- Chicken Bouillon Cubes
- Chicken Stock
- Cilantro
- Garlic Paste
- Garlic Powder
- Garlic Salt
- Green Onions
- Hoisin Sauce
- Jerk Seasoning
- Mrs. Dash
- Old Bay Seasoning
- Onion Powder

- Onion Salt
- Oregano
- Paprika
- Parsley
- Salt (kosher & sea salt)
- Scotch Bonnet/Habanero
- Soy Sauce
- Sriracha Sauce
- Thyme
- Tomato Bouillon Cubes
- White Onions

Essential Cookware

- Baking Sheet
- Blender
- Cake Pan
- Casserole Dish
- Cast Iron Pan
- Cutting Board
- Dutch Pot
- Frying Pan
- Griddle Pan
- Mixing Bowl
- Saucepan
- Sauté Pan
- Stock Pot
- Strainer
- Wok

Necessary Utensils

- Aluminum Foil
- Blender
- Can Opener
- Chef's Knife
- Grater
- Hand Mixer
- Ladle
- Measuring Cups
- Measuring Spoons
- Meat Cleaver
- Oven Mitt
- Parchment Paper
- Peeler
- Potato Masher
- Silicone Utensils
- Spatulas
- Thermometer
- Tongs
- Whisk

Brunchin'

RED-VELVET PANCAKES WITH CREAM CHEESE ICING

For the Cream Cheese Icing

- ½ cup of Powdered Sugar
- ⅔ cup of Heavy Whipping Cream
- 4-ounces of Cream Cheese (half of a cream cheese packet)

For the Pancakes

- 2 cups Flour
- 3 tablespoons of Sugar
- 1 ½ teaspoons Baking Powder
- 1 ½ Baking Soda
- 2 tablespoons of Coco Powder
- ¼ teaspoon of Kosher Salt
- ½ cup Powdered Sugar
- 2 Large Eggs
- 1 teaspoon of Vanilla
- 2 cups Milk
- 5 tablespoons Melted Butter
- 2 teaspoons Red Food Coloring
- Nonstick Spray

TOTAL TIME 20 MINUTES

SERVES 6

FOR THE CREAM CHEESE ICING

STEP 1. Combine the powdered sugar, heavy whipping cream, and cream cheese in a mixing bowl. Use a large spoon or fork to whip the ingredients for 1-2 minutes. Set the icing aside for now. You will finish off the pancakes with it later.

FOR THE PANCAKES

STEP 2. Combine the dry ingredients (flour, sugar, baking powder, baking soda, coco powder, salt, and powdered sugar) in a mixing bowl. Mix all the dry ingredients well.

STEP 3. Make a well in the center of the dry ingredients then crack the eggs into the dry ingredients' mixing bowl. Add in the wet ingredients (vanilla, milk, butter, food coloring) to the bowl. Whisk all of ingredients together to create the pancake batter.

STEP 4. Coat a skillet with nonstick spray then place over medium heat. Pour in the batter half a cup at a time.

STEP 5. When bubbles cover the surface of the pancake, it is ready to flip. DO NOT flip until the batter has set in (bubbled). Flip the pancake with a spatula. The top side of the pancake should be golden brown, and the edges should have a slight crisp. Continue cooking on the other side for 2-4 minutes.

STEP 6. Once the pancakes have finished, drizzle the cream cheese icing over them. Serve with pancake syrup.

GRANNY'S OLD-FASHIONED BUTTERMILK PANCAKES

- 2 cups Flour
- 5 tablespoons of Sugar
- 3 teaspoons Baking Powder
- 2 teaspoons Baking Soda
- ⅛ teaspoon of Salt
- ½ cup Powdered Sugar
- 5 tablespoons Melted Butter
- 2 teaspoons Vanilla Extract
- 3 cups Buttermilk
- 3 Eggs
- Nonstick spray

TOTAL TIME 20 MINUTES

SERVES 6

STEP 1. Combine the dry ingredients (flour, sugar, baking powder, baking soda, salt, powdered sugar) in a mixing bowl. Mix all dry ingredients well.

STEP 2. Make a well in the middle of the dry ingredients then add the wet ingredients (butter, vanilla, buttermilk, eggs) to the mixing bowl. Whisk the ingredients to create the pancake batter.

STEP 3. Coat a skillet with nonstick spray then place over medium heat. Pour in the batter half a cup at a time.

STEP 4. When bubbles cover the surface of the pancake, it is ready to flip. DO NOT flip until the batter has set in (bubbled). Flip the pancake with a spatula. The top side of the pancake should be golden brown, and the edges should have a slight crisp. Continue cooking on the other side for 2-4 minutes.

STEP 5. Serve hot with pancake syrup and fresh fruit.

NOTE: For crispy edges, add a half tablespoon of oil to the pot before each pancake.

BLUEBERRY BANANA PANCAKES

- 3 teaspoons Baking Powder
- 2 teaspoons Baking Soda
- 2 cups Flour
- 5 tablespoons of Sugar
- ⅛ teaspoon Salt
- 3 Eggs
- 4 Ripe Bananas (Mashed)
- 3 cups Buttermilk
- 5 tablespoons Melted Butter
- 2 teaspoons Vanilla Extract
- 2 ½ cups Blueberries
- Nonstick spray

TOTAL TIME 20 MINUTES

SERVES 6

NOTE: You can add blueberries to the top of the batter after pouring it into the skillet rather than mixing them into the batter.

STEP 1. With a whisk or fork, combine the dry ingredients in a mixing bowl (baking powder, baking soda, flour, sugar, and salt).

STEP 2. Crack the eggs into the mixing bowl then add in the wet ingredients (mashed bananas, buttermilk, melted butter, and vanilla extract). Whisk the ingredients together until they form a pourable batter.

STEP 3. Rinse the blueberries then stir them into the batter.

STEP 4. Coat a skillet with nonstick spray then place over medium heat. Pour in the batter half a cup at a time.

STEP 5. When bubbles cover the surface of the pancake, it is ready to flip. DO NOT flip until the batter has set in (bubbled). Flip the pancake with a spatula. The top side of the pancake should be golden brown, and the edges should have a slight crisp. Continue cooking on the other side for 2-4 minutes.

STEP 6. Serve hot with pancake syrup.

APPLE CINNAMON FRENCH TOAST

FOR THE EGG MIXTURE

STEP 1. Crack the eggs into a mixing bowl, then pour in the milk, and vanilla extract. Lightly beat the egg mixture, then sprinkle in the cinnamon, nutmeg, and sugar. Continue whisking the mixture until the ingredients are well combined.

STEP 2. Dip the French bread into the egg mixture and allow the excess to drip off. Add butter to the pan. Toast the French bread over medium heat for 2-3 minutes on each side or until golden-brown and crispy. Remove from the pan and rest on a serving plate.

FOR THE CINNAMON APPLES

STEP 3. Place the apples into a small pot over medium low heat. Add butter, then sprinkle in the cinnamon, nutmeg, brown sugar, and vanilla. Cook for 3-5 minutes.

STEP 4. Pour the hot cinnamon apples over the French toast. Dust powdered sugar over the top and serve immediately.

NOTE: Slice bread in half diagonally

- Loaf of French Toast Bread

FOR THE EGG MIXTURE

- 3 Eggs
- ½ cup Milk
- ¼ teaspoon Vanilla Extract
- ¼ teaspoon Cinnamon
- ⅛ teaspoon Nutmeg
- 2 ½ tablespoons Sugar

FOR THE CINNAMON APPLES

- 2-3 Apples, peeled and sliced
- 1 teaspoon Butter
- ½ teaspoon Cinnamon
- Pinch Nutmeg
- ⅛ cup Brown Sugar
- Splash Vanilla Extract

TOTAL TIME 20 MINUTES

SERVES 4

VERY BERRY STUFFED FRENCH TOAST

- Loaf of French Toast Bread

FOR THE CREAM CHEESE ICING

- 4 ounces Cream Cheese (half of a cream cheese packet)
- ½ cup Powdered Sugar
- 2/3 cup Heavy Whipping Cream

FOR THE EGG MIXTURE

- 3 Eggs
- ½ cup Milk
- ¼ teaspoon Vanilla Extract
- ¼ teaspoon Cinnamon
- ⅛ teaspoon Nutmeg
- 2 ½ tablespoons Sugar

FOR THE BERRY COMPOTE

- ½ cup Strawberries, chopped
- ½ cup Raspberries
- ½ cup Blueberries
- ¼ cup Heavy Whipping Cream
- ½ teaspoon Vanilla Extract
- ½ teaspoon Cinnamon
- ¼ teaspoon Nutmeg
- 1 teaspoon Brown Sugar
- 1 teaspoon White Sugar

TOTAL TIME 20 MINUTES

SERVES 4

FOR THE CREAM CHEESE ICING

STEP 1. Add the cream cheese, powdered sugar, and heavy whipping cream in a mixing bowl. Use a large spoon to stir the ingredients until they are thoroughly combined.

STEP 2. Spread a generous amount of the cream cheese icing on two slices of bread. Sandwich the two slices together with the cream cheese sides facing each other.

FOR THE EGG MIXTURE

STEP 3. Crack the eggs into a mixing bowl, then pour in the milk, and vanilla extract. Lightly beat the egg mixture then add cinnamon, nutmeg, and sugar, and continue beating until all the ingredients are combined.

STEP 4. Dip the French bread into the egg mixture and allow the excess to drip off. Add butter to the pan. Toast the French bread over medium heat for 2-3 minutes on each side or until golden-brown and crispy. Remove from the pan and rest on a serving plate.
For the Berry Compote

STEP 5. In a medium-sized pot, add all berries, heavy whipping cream, vanilla extract, cinnamon, nutmeg, brown sugar, and white sugar. Simmer on low heat, stir continuously until the mixture has thickened.

STEP 6. Pour the berries over the French toast. Dust powdered sugar over the top and serve immediately.

NOTE: Slice bread in half diagonally

BRIOCHE FRENCH TOAST

FOR THE EGG MIXTURE

STEP 1. Crack the eggs into a mixing bowl, then pour in the milk, and vanilla extract. Lightly beat the egg mixture then add the cinnamon, nutmeg, and sugar. Continue beating until all the ingredients are combined.

STEP 2. Preheat butter in a skillet over medium heat. Dip the French bread into the egg mixture and allow the excess to drip off. Toast the French bread on each side for 2-3 minutes or until golden brown and crispy. Remove from the pan and rest on a serving plate.

STEP 3. Sprinkle a pinch of brown sugar over each slice of toast before serving.

NOTE: Slice bread in half diagonally

FOR THE EGG MIXTURE

- 3 Eggs
- ½ cup Milk
- ¼ teaspoon Vanilla Extract
- ¼ teaspoon Cinnamon
- ⅛ teaspoon Nutmeg
- 2 ½ tablespoons Sugar

FOR THE BREAD

- Loaf of French Toast Bread
- 1 teaspoon Butter
- Brown Sugar (add to preference)

TOTAL TIME 15 MINUTES

SERVES 4

PORRIDGE

- 4 cups Water
- 1 ½ teaspoons Cinnamon
- 2 teaspoons Vanilla
- ½ teaspoon of Nutmeg
- 1 cup of Old-Fashioned Oats
- 3 tablespoons of Sweet Condensed Milk
- ¼ cup of White Sugar
- 1 tablespoon Butter

TOTAL TIME 30 MINUTES

SERVES 4

STEP 1. Bring a pot of water to boil. Add the cinnamon, vanilla, and nutmeg to the pot then stir the ingredients for 1-2 minutes.

STEP 2. Pour in the old-fashioned oats then set the heat to medium. Simmer the oats for 15-20 minutes, stirring occasionally.

STEP 3. Pour in the condensed milk and sugar. Continue to stir the ingredients. Let oats simmer for 1-2 more minutes. Turn off the heat and stir in the butter before serving.

SHRIMP N' GRITS

FOR THE GRITS

- ¾ cup Grits
- 3 cups Water
- 2 tablespoons of Butter

FOR THE SHRIMP

- 2-pounds of Shrimp, peeled and deveined
- 1 tablespoon Cajun seasoning
- ½ tablespoon Italian seasoning
- ¾ of a tablespoon Old Bay seasoning
- ⅛ teaspoon of Cayenne pepper
- ⅛ teaspoon of Paprika
- ⅛ cup of Cilantro
- ⅛ cup of Parsley
- 1 ½ cups of Chicken stock
- 1 Green Bell Peppers, chopped
- 1 Red Bell Peppers, chopped

FOR THE CORNSTARCH SLURRY

- 1 teaspoon Cornstarch
- 2 teaspoons Water

TOTAL TIME 30 MINUTES

SERVES 4

FOR THE GRITS

STEP 1. Add the grits to a medium-sized saucepan over medium heat then pour in the water. Toss the butter into the pan and stir the mixture well.

STEP 2. Cover the saucepan and simmer the grits, stirring occasionally. Simmer for 30-40 minutes or until the grits have thickened.

FOR THE SHRIMP

STEP 3. In a mixing bowl, season the shrimp with Cajun seasoning, Italian seasoning, Old Bay seasoning, cayenne pepper, paprika, cilantro, and parsley.

STEP 4. Sauté the shrimp in a sauté pan until it is halfway cooked. Pour in the chicken stock. Combine the ingredients for the cornstarch slurry in a small bowl then gradually stir it into the sauce. Continue to stir until the sauce thickens. Cook the shrimp for 8-10 minutes over low heat, stirring occasionally.

STEP 5. Plate the grits first. Once the shrimp has cooked through (it should be saucy), pour the shrimp over the grits and serve.

BAGEL BREAKFAST SLIDES

- 4 Sausage Patties
- 4 Eggs
- 2 teaspoon Butter, separated
- 4 Bagels
- 4 Slices of Cheddar Cheese

TOTAL TIME 12-15 MINUTES

SERVES 4

STEP 1. Preheat the oven to 400ºF. Cook the sausage patties in the skillet over medium heat until they are well done.

STEP 2. Crack the eggs into a bowl, then whisk. Warm the butter in a skillet over medium heat then pour in the eggs. Scramble the eggs to your preferred texture. Remove the eggs from the heat.

STEP 3. Warm a teaspoon of butter in a skillet over medium heat. Slice the bagels into halves then toast them on both sides.

STEP 4. It's time to build the sandwiches! First, place a portion of eggs on the bottom half of each bagel. Top the eggs with the sausage patty, next add the cheese, then the top with the other half of the bagel.

STEP 5. Lay the bagel sandwiches on a baking sheet then place them in the oven to toast and melt the cheese. Keep a close eye, remove quickly to ensure they do not burn. Cool before serving.

CROISSANT BREAKFAST SANDWICH

STEP 1. Preheat the oven to 400ºF. Cut the sausages in half. Place the bacon and sausages onto a baking sheet then season with black pepper. Place the bacon and sausages into the oven and bake for 15 minutes.

STEP 2. Beat the eggs then pour them into a skillet, toss in the spinach. Season with black pepper then scramble the eggs and spinach until cooked through.

STEP 3. Cut the croissants in half. Using a knife, spread butter onto each half.

STEP 4. Build the sandwiches by placing a portion of eggs on the bottom half of each croissant first. Top the eggs with the bacon and sausages. next add cheese, then the top half of the croissant.

STEP 5. Spread butter and drizzle honey over the top of the croissants. Place the sandwiches into the oven to toast for 5 minutes. Remove promptly.

STEP 6. Plate the croissants and serve immediately.

- 4 slices Bacon
- 4 sausages
- Black Pepper, to taste
- 4 Eggs
- 1 cup of Spinach
- 4 Croissants
- 1 tablespoon Butter
- Shredded Cheese, (add to preference)
- Honey, (add to preference)

TOTAL TIME 30 MINUTES

SERVES 4

BREAKFAST BURRITO

- 4 Turkey Sausage Patties
- 4 Eggs
- 1 cup Spinach
- ½ teaspoon of Black Pepper
- ½ teaspoon of Garlic Powder
- ½ teaspoon of Garlic Salt
- 4 Medium Flour Tortillas
- Shredded Cheese, to preference
- Olive Oil, to coat the pan
- Salsa, to preference

TOTAL TIME 15-20 MINUTES

SERVES 4-6

STEP 1. Warm a frying pan over medium-high heat then cook and scramble the sausage for 7-8 minutes.

STEP 2. Crack the eggs into a bowl then whisk them until well beaten. Pour the eggs into the frying pan with the sausage then scramble and cook them until almost done. Add the spinach then sprinkle in some black pepper, garlic powder, and garlic salt. Wilt the spinach and cook the eggs to your desired consistency. Remove the egg scramble from the heat.

STEP 3. Warm a pan over medium heat. Warm the tortilla on each side. Remove the tortilla, place it on a serving plate.

STEP 4. Fill the tortilla with the egg scramble then sprinkle shredded cheese over top. Roll the tortilla into a burrito by folding the sides inward then fold the bottom of the tortilla over the two folded sides and roll upwards. Add olive oil to the pan and toast the burrito for 2-3 minutes on each side. Serve hot with salsa.

CHICKEN APPLE BREAKFAST HASH

STEP 1. Warm the olive oil in a large sauté pan over medium-high heat. Toss in the potatoes and cook for 15-20 minutes, then add the bell peppers to the pan. Cook until tender, about 15 minutes.

STEP 2. In a separate pan, add olive oil and add egg sunny side up, and cook to over hard or over medium.

STEP 3. Once the potatoes are tender, add the chopped chicken apple sausage. Season with paprika,
garlic salt, garlic powder, onion powder, and parsley. Continue to sauté for 3-5 minutes. Then place egg over it, and serve.

STEP 4. Remove the hash from the pan and garnish with parsley. Serve hot.

- 3 tablespoons Olive Oil
- 6 Gold Potatoes, diced
- ¼ cup Green Bell Peppers, diced
- ¼ cup Red Bell Peppers, diced
- ¼ cup Orange Bell Peppers, diced
- ¼ cup Yellow Bell Peppers, diced
- 3 Chicken Apple Sausage Links, chopped
- 1 Egg
- ½ teaspoon Paprika
- 1 teaspoon Garlic Salt
- ½ teaspoon Garlic Powder
- ½ teaspoon Onion Powder
- 1 teaspoon Parsley

TOTAL TIME 30 MINUTES

SERVES 6

HOME FRIES

- 3 tablespoons Olive Oil
- 8-9 Small Russet Potatoes, large diced
- ¼ teaspoon Paprika
- 1 teaspoon Garlic salt
- ¼ teaspoon Black Pepper
- 1 teaspoon Seasoned Salt
- 1 teaspoon Parsley
- 1 Green Bell Pepper, chopped
- 1 Red Bell Pepper, chopped
- 1 Orange Bell Pepper, chopped
- 1 White Onion, chopped

TOTAL TIME 15 MINUTES

SERVES 5-6

STEP 1. Warm olive oil in a skillet over medium-high heat. Sauté the potatoes in olive oil for about 1 minute. Add all of the seasonings (paprika, garlic salt, black pepper, seasoned salt, and parsley. Continue to cook and brown the potatoes for another 2-3 minutes.

STEP 2. Add the bell peppers and white onions, then continue to cook the potatoes for about 10 minutes or until they have softened to fork tender.

STEP 3. Remove the potatoes from the heat. Serve garnished with a sprinkle of sea salt.

WHENEVER SOMEONE ASKS WHAT MY PASSION IS, I SAY FASHION IS MY FIRST LOVE, BUT COOKING IS WHERE MY HEART IS.

OMELET

- Olive Oil, to coat the bottom of the pan
- 4 slices of Bacon
- 2 Sausages
- 1 cup Pre Cooked Potatoes, diced
- ¼ cup of Red Bell Peppers
- ¼ cup of Orange Bell Peppers
- 1 tablespoon White Onion
- 1 teaspoon All-Purpose Seasoning
- 2 cups Spinach
- 1 teaspoon Butter
- 6 Eggs
- Mexican Blend Shredded Cheese, to preference

TOTAL TIME 15 MINUTES
SERVES 2

STEP 1. Heat the olive oil in a sauté pan. Meanwhile, chop the bacon and sausage before putting it into the pan. Sauté.

STEP 2. Add the potatoes to the pan, along with the peppers and onions. Season with all-purpose seasoning and cook for about 8-10 minutes. Add the chopped bacon and sausage. Cook for another 5 minutes. Add in the spinach and cook for 3-4 minutes. Set aside.

STEP 3. Heat butter in a separate skillet over medium heat. Beat the eggs in a bowl, then pour out half into the skillet – half for each omelet. Once the eggs have thickened at the bottom of the pan, sprinkle the cheese on one side of the omelet.

STEP 4. On the same side that the cheese was added to, add the bacon, sausage, potatoes, spinach, and onions, being careful to not overfill the omelet. Flip the other side of the omelet over the filling. Once the egg is cooked through, remove it from the pan and garnish with parsley.

BISCUITS N' GRAVY

- 1-pound bag of Biscuits, frozen
- 1 ½ tablespoons Butter
- 1 (10 ounce) bag of Turkey Sausage Crumbles
- 3 cups Heavy Whipping Cream
- 2 ½ cups Half & Half Milk
- Flour (1 tsp at a time)
- ½ teaspoon Black Pepper
- ½ tablespoon Garlic Salt
- ½ teaspoon Seasoned Salt
- ½ tablespoon Parsley

TOTAL TIME 20 MINUTES
SERVES 6

STEP 1. Preheat the oven and follow the package instructions for baking the biscuits.

STEP 2. Meanwhile, warm the butter in a saucepan over medium heat. Add the turkey sausage crumbles. Sauté for 6-8 minutes.

STEP 3. Pour in heavy whipping cream and half and half milk. Whisk while gradually adding flour until the mixture thickens into a gravy.

STEP 4. While stirring the gravy, season with black pepper, garlic salt, seasoned salt, and parsley. Simmer for 3-5 minutes, stirring occasionally.

STEP 5. Arrange the biscuits onto a serving plate then pour gravy over top before serving.

Krav'n
CARBS

CAJUN CHICKEN ALFREDO

FOR THE CHICKEN

- 1 ½ pounds Chicken Breast Tenders, cube diced
- 1 teaspoon Minced Garlic
- 1 teaspoon Old Bay Seasoning
- 1 teaspoon Garlic Powder
- 1 teaspoon Cajun Seasoning
- ½ teaspoon Black Pepper
- ⅛ teaspoon Cayenne pepper
- 1teaspoon Blackened Seasoning
- 1 tablespoon Olive Oil

FOR THE SAUCE

- ⅛ cup Parsley, chopped
- ⅛ cup Cilantro chopped
- 3 cloves Fresh Garlic, chopped
- 2 cups Heavy Whipping Cream
- 1 ¼ cup Parmesan Cheese
- 1 ¼ cup Mozzarella Cheese
- 1 teaspoon Blackened Seasoning
- ¼ teaspoon Cayenne Pepper
- ⅛ teaspoon Garlic Salt

FOR THE PASTA

- Pinch of Salt
- 1-pound box Fettucine Pasta
- 1 tablespoon Olive Oil
- ¼ teaspoon Garlic Salt
- 1 stick Butter, unsalted

TOTAL TIME 30-35 MINUTES

SERVES 10-14

FOR THE CHICKEN

STEP 1. Rinse the chicken with a mix of white vinegar and water. Place the chicken in a mixing bowl and season with minced garlic, Old Bay seasoning, garlic powder, Cajun seasoning, black pepper, cayenne pepper, and blackened seasoning.

STEP 2. Warm the olive oil in a sauté pan, then add the chicken. Cook the chicken for 12-15 minutes or until cooked through. Remove the chicken from the pan and set it aside.

FOR THE SAUCE

STEP 3. Sauté the parsley, cilantro, and garlic in a sauté pan over medium-low heat. Pour in the heavy cream then bring to a slow simmer. Whisk in the parmesan and mozzarella cheeses, half a cup at a time. The sauce will begin to thicken. Sprinkle in the blackened seasoning, cayenne pepper, and garlic salt, then stir well. Allow the sauce to continue thickening to a creamy consistency; at least 30 minutes.

FOR THE PASTA

STEP 4. Boil a pot of water with a pinch of salt. Add a tablespoon of olive oil, to keep the pasta from sticking. Toss in the pasta and boil for roughly 6 minutes or until the pasta is al dente.

STEP 5. Drain the pasta water. Add garlic salt and butter to the pasta, then toss to combine well.

STEP 6. Combine the pasta with the sauce in the sauté pan, then add the chicken. Cover and simmer for 10-15 minutes over low heat.

STEP 7. Plate the pasta and garnish with a sprinkle of Cajun seasoning and parsley.

TURKEY SPAGHETTI

STEP 1. Place the ground turkey into a saucepan over medium-low heat then add parsley, bell peppers, and white onions. Cook for 10 minutes or until the turkey has cooked through.

STEP 2. Stir in the crushed tomatoes and add all of the seasonings (cumin, garlic powder, Italian seasoning, onion powder, garlic salt, cayenne pepper, and crushed red pepper).

STEP 3. Boil the pasta in a medium-sized pot with a pinch of salt and olive oil.

STEP 4. Pour in the tomato paste and tomato sauce. Cover the pan and simmer for 10 minutes.

STEP 5. Drain the pasta noodles in a strainer. Plate the noodles then top them with meat sauce. You are ready to serve!

- 1-pound of Ground Turkey
- ⅓ cup Parsley
- 1 ½ cups Tri-Colored Bell Peppers, diced
- ½ cup White Onions, diced
- 1 (28-ounce) can Crushed Tomatoes
- ¼ teaspoon Cumin
- ¼ teaspoon Garlic Powder
- ½ tablespoon Italian Seasoning
- ⅛ teaspoon Onion Powder
- A dash Garlic Salt
- ⅛ teaspoon Cayenne Pepper
- ¼ teaspoon Crushed Red Pepper
- 2-pounds of Spaghetti Pasta Noodles
- pinch of Salt
- ½ teaspoon Olive Oil
- 1 (6-ounce) can Tomato Paste
- ⅓ cup Tomato Sauce

TOTAL TIME 25-30 MINUTES

SERVES 8

EXTRA CHEESY TURKEY LASAGNA

- Shredded Cheese, (add to preference, at least 1 ½ lbs)

FOR THE PASTA

- 2-pound box Lasagna Pasta Noodles
- pinch of Himalayan Salt
- ½ teaspoon Olive Oil

FOR THE MEAT SAUCE

- 1 cup White Onions, chopped
- 1 tablespoon Parsley
- 2-pounds of Ground Turkey (Ground Beef, optional)
- 4 cloves Garlic, chopped
- 1 (24 ounce) can Crushed Tomatoes
- 1 (6 ounce) can Tomato Paste
- ½ teaspoon Black Pepper
- 2 tablespoons Oregano
- ½ tablespoon Fennel Seed
- ¼ teaspoon Garlic Salt
- ¼ teaspoon Cayenne Pepper

FOR THE RICOTTA MIX

- 3 cups Ricotta Cheese
- 1 tablespoon Garlic Paste
- ½ cup Parsley
- ½ cup Parmesan, grated
- ¼ teaspoon Garlic Salt
- ¼ teaspoon Black Pepper
- 2 Eggs

TOTAL TIME 45-50 MINUTES

SERVES 8-10

FOR THE PASTA

STEP 1. Preheat the oven to 400ºF. Boil the lasagna noodles in a pot with a pinch of Himalayan salt and olive oil. Cook until the noodles are al dente, they will finish cooking in the oven.

FOR THE MEAT SAUCE

STEP 2. In a medium-sized pot, add onions and parsley. Sauté for 1 minute, then add the ground turkey and garlic into the pot. Using a wooden spoon, crumble the ground turkey then sauté until it has cooked thoroughly.

STEP 3. Stir in crushed tomatoes and tomato paste. Season with black pepper, oregano, fennel seed, garlic salt, and cayenne pepper. Cover the pot and simmer the meat sauce for 30 minutes.

FOR THE RICOTTA MIX

STEP 4. Place the Ricotta cheese into a large bowl, then mix in the garlic paste, parsley, grated parmesan, garlic salt, black pepper, and two cracked eggs. Combine well.

STEP 5. Spread a thin layer of meat sauce evenly along the bottom of a 12-inch casserole dish so the noodles don't stick. Next, place a layer of noodles over the sauce. The noodles can overlap. Spread a thick layer of the ricotta cheese mix on top of the pasta, then pour on a thick layer of meat sauce. Sprinkle shredded cheese over the meat sauce.

STEP 6. Repeat this step twice more, but do not add ricotta cheese on the last layer (there should only be two layers of ricotta cheese).

STEP 7. Cover the casserole dish with foil then bake for 35-40 minutes. Remove the lasagna from the oven and carefully uncover. Place it back in the oven for 5 minutes to brown the cheese.

STEP 8. The dish will be very hot, be careful removing it from the oven. Cool for at least 15 minutes. To cut each portion, slice through all layers of the lasagna with a chef's knife. Use a metal or rubber spatula to remove each serving.

SEAFOOD LINGUINE

FOR THE CRAB

- 3 cloves Garlic
- 1 slice of Lemon
- 1 teaspoon Fresh Cilantro
- 1 teaspoon Fresh Parsley
- 4 clusters Snow Crab

FOR THE PASTA

- 1-pound box Linguine Pasta Noodles
- pinch of Himalayan salt
- ½ teaspoon Olive Oil

FOR THE SAUCE

- ½ teaspoon Olive Oil
- 2-pounds Shrimp, peeled and deveined
- 2 cups White Cooking Wine
- 4 tablespoons Butter
- 1 tablespoon Cilantro
- 1 tablespoon Minced Garlic
- ½ tablespoon Garlic Powder
- ½ tablespoon Mrs. Dash
- ½ tablespoon Parsley

TOTAL TIME 30 MINUTES

SERVES 8-10

FOR THE CRAB

STEP 1. Boil the garlic cloves, a slice of lemon, cilantro, and parsley in a large pot of water over high heat for 5-10 minutes. Place the snow crab clusters into the water then reduce the heat to a simmer and cook for 15 minutes.

FOR THE PASTA

STEP 2. While the snow crab cluster is simmering, boil the pasta with a pinch of Himalayan salt and ½ teaspoon of olive oil in a separate pot. Cook for 5-8 minutes or until al dente.

FOR THE SAUCE

STEP 3. Sauté the shrimp with the olive oil in a sauté pan over medium heat for 5-8 minutes.

STEP 4. Remove the shrimp from the sauté pan and set aside. Pour in the white cooking wine, then add the butter, cilantro, minced garlic, garlic powder, Mrs. Dash, and parsley to the sauté pan. Cook over medium-high heat for 5-8 minutes.

STEP 5. Drain the pasta in a strainer then add to the sauce. Turn the heat to medium then mix well, ensuring that the sauce fully coats the noodles.

STEP 6. Use tongs to toss in the shrimp. Cook for 1-2 minutes then add the crab cluster. Serve garnished with fresh parsley and lemon.

SPICY RAMEN

- 3 Cups Water
- ½ stick of Butter
- 1 tablespoon Minced Garlic
- 1 tablespoon Parsley
- 2 – 3 tablespoons Soy Sauce (or to preference)
- 1 tablespoon Paprika
- 1 tablespoon Sriracha sauce
- 1 tablespoon Worcestershire Sauce
- 4 Packs of Ramen Noodles
- 1 Chicken Bouillon Cube

TOTAL TIME 10 MINUTES

SERVES 4

STEP 1. Bring the water to a boil in a large pot. Add butter, minced garlic, parsley, soy sauce, paprika, Sriracha sauce, and Worcestershire sauce to the pot. Stir to combine well.

STEP 2. Add the ramen noodles and a chicken bouillon cube. DO NOT add the seasoning packets from the ramen noodle package. Boil the noodles for 4 minutes over medium-high heat.

STEP 3. Serve immediately after the ramen has cooked, and the broth is hot and steamy.

STUFFED PASTA SHELLS

- pinch of Himalayan Salt
- 6 ounces (Half of a 12-ounce box) of Jumbo Pasta Shells
- 1 cup White Onions, diced
- 4 cups Spinach
- 1 tablespoon Minced Garlic
- ¼ teaspoon Oregano
- 2 ½ tablespoons Parsley, chopped
- ¼ teaspoon Black Pepper
- ¼ teaspoon Garlic Powder
- ¼ tablespoon Garlic Salt
- 2 cups Ricotta Cheese
- ⅓ cup of Parmesan Cheese, grated
- ⅓ cup of Italian Blend Cheese, shredded
- Marinara Sauce (about 2 cups or to preference)

TOTAL TIME 35 MINUTES

SERVES 4

STEP 1. Preheat the oven to 350ºF. Bring a large pot of water to boil then add a pinch of Himalayan Salt. Pour in the pasta shells and give them a stir. Cover the pot and cook the pasta to al dente. The pasta shells should have some firmness for easier stuffing. Drain the pasta water using a strainer. Shock the pasta by rinsing it with cold water to stop the cooking process. Set the pasta shells aside.

STEP 2. Sauté the white onions, spinach, and minced garlic in a sauté pan over medium-high heat. Cook until the spinach has wilted down to slightly over 1 cup.

STEP 3. Season with oregano, parsley, black pepper, garlic powder, and garlic salt. Stir all three cheeses into the spinach mixture. Mix well to fully combine the filling.

STEP 4. Spread a generous layer of marinara sauce in the bottom of a glass baking dish. Stuff each pasta shell with two tablespoons of filling, then place them into the baking dish.

STEP 5. Cover the baking dish with foil. Bake the stuffed pasta shells for 15 minutes. Uncover the baking dish, then bake for another 10 minutes. Remove from the oven and allow to cool for 2-3 minutes, then serve.

ITALIAN DIJON CHICKEN PASTA

FOR THE CHICKEN

- 2-pounds Chicken Breast Tenderloins, diced
- 1 tablespoon Mrs. Dash Original Blend
- ½ tablespoon Minced Garlic
- ½ tablespoon Cilantro
- ½ tablespoon Parsley
- ¼ teaspoon Onion Powder
- ¼ teaspoon Black Pepper

FOR THE PASTA

- 4 quarts Water
- 1 tablespoon Himalayan Salt
- 1 (16-ounce) Penne Pasta

FOR THE SAUCE

- 3 tablespoon Olive Oil
- ½ cup Sundried Tomatoes
- 2 ½ cups Heavy Whipping Cream
- ⅓ cup Italian Dressing
- ⅛ cup Dijon Mustard
- 6 cups Spinach

TOTAL TIME 35 MINUTES

SERVES 4

FOR THE CHICKEN

STEP 1. Place the chicken into a large bowl along with Mrs. Dash, minced garlic, cilantro, parsley, onion powder, and black pepper. Mix well to fully coat the chicken with seasoning.

FOR THE PASTA

STEP 2. In a separate pot, add four quarts of water and a tablespoon of Himalayan salt. Boil the pasta to al dente. Drain. Add butter and garlic salt then mix thoroughly.

FOR THE SAUCE

STEP 3. Heat olive oil in a separate pot. Sauté the chicken on medium heat until cooked through.

STEP 4. Add sun-dried tomatoes, heavy whipping cream, Italian dressing, Dijon mustard, and spinach. Mix.

STEP 5. Add pasta to chicken and sauce, mix, then serve.

Meat
BY THE SEA

BLACKENED SALMON

- 6 (6-ounce) Salmon Fillets
- Minced Garlic, a light coat over each fillet
- Mrs. Dash, to taste
- Cajun seasoning, to taste (optional)
- Blackened seasoning, to taste

TOTAL TIME: 15 MINUTES

SERVES: 6

STEP 1. Rinse the salmon with a mix of white vinegar and water. Pat dry with a paper towel. Lay the salmon fillets on a clean, flat, surface to be seasoned. Rub minced garlic over the top and bottom of the fillets.

STEP 2. Season both sides of the fillets with Mrs. Dash, Cajun seasoning, and blackened seasoning. Season to your liking.

STEP 3. In the grill pan, grill the salmon over medium-high heat for 10 minutes or until cooked through.

NOTE: You will need a grill pan. (The salmon can be baked or grilled for 10 minutes. If you prefer to bake, preheat the oven to 400ºF.)

I LOVE COOKING FOR THE SAME REASON THAT I LOVE FASHION – THE THRILL OF CREATING SOMETHING NEW.

SALMON CROQUETTES

FOR THE SALMON

STEP 1. Place the salmon into a large mixing bowl. Using your hands, crumble the salmon while also removing all bones, fat, and skin.

STEP 2. Season the salmon with black pepper, onion powder, minced garlic, onion salt, Old Bay seasoning, and garlic powder.

STEP 3. In a separate bowl, crack two eggs then whisk them. Pour the whisked eggs into the mixing bowl along with the mayonnaise. Using your hands, mix until well combined.

STEP 4. Shape the salmon croquettes by placing ¼ cup of the mixture into your hand and then use both hands to squeeze it into a ball. Next, gently flatten the ball into the thickness you desire. Pour Panko breadcrumbs into a bowl and then fully coat the croquettes.

STEP 5. Heat the vegetable oil in a sauté pan over medium-high heat. Place the croquettes in the hot oil and fry for 6 minutes on each side. Place on a cooling rack for 1-2 minutes to drain all excess oil, serve while still warm.

FOR THE SALMON

- 2 (14.75-ounce) cans of Pink Salmon
- ¼ teaspoon Black Pepper
- ½ teaspoon Onion Powder
- 1 tablespoon Minced Garlic
- ¼ teaspoon Onion Salt
- ½ tablespoon Old Bay seasoning
- ½ tablespoon Garlic Powder
- 2 Eggs
- 1 tablespoon Mayonnaise
- ¼ cup White Onions, chopped
- ½ cup Panko Breadcrumbs
- 2 cups Vegetable Oil

TOTAL TIME 15 MINUTES

SERVES 10

GARLIC ROSEMARY LAMB CHOPS

FOR THE MARINADE

- 1 ½ tablespoon Parsley
- 1 ½ tablespoon Cilantro
- 1 tablespoon Thyme
- 1 tablespoon Minced Garlic
- ½ tablespoon Black Pepper
- 1 teaspoon Garlic Salt
- 1 tablespoon Onion Powder

FOR THE LAMB

- Full Rack of Lamb
- 3 tablespoons Olive Oil
- 3 springs Rosemary

TOTAL TIME 40 MINUTES

SERVES 4

FOR THE MARINADE

STEP 1. Add the parsley, cilantro, thyme, minced garlic, black pepper, garlic salt, and onion powder to a large mixing bowl. Create the marinade by whisking together the ingredients until thoroughly combined.

FOR THE LAMB

STEP 2. Coat both sides of the rack of lamb with the marinade then slice the lamb into chops. Allow the lamb chops to marinate, covered, for 30 minutes.

STEP 3. Preheat the oven to 350ºF. Meanwhile, drizzle olive oil in a large, heavy-bottomed skillet. Position the skillet over medium-high heat. Sear each side of the lamb chops for 2-3 minutes.

STEP 4. Place the lamb chops into a baking pan with the sprigs of Rosemary. Finish off the lamb in the oven for 5-6 minutes.

STEP 5. Remove the lamb chops from the oven and allow them to rest for 1-2 minutes before serving.

STUFFED SALMON

FOR THE FILLER

- 1 ½ cups Frozen Spinach
- 1 (12-ounce) Cream Cheese pack
- ½ cup Parmesan Cheese, shredded
- ¼ teaspoon Black Pepper
- ⅛ teaspoon Garlic Salt
- ½ tablespoon Garlic Paste
- 1 teaspoon Cilantro or Parsley

FOR THE SALMON

- 6 (6-8 ounce) Salmon fillets
- 1 tablespoon Mrs. Dash

TOTAL TIME 15 MINUTES

SERVES 4-6

NOTE: The cream cheese should be at room temperature and the frozen spinach should be thawed before you begin.

FOR THE FILLER

STEP 1. Preheat the oven to 400ºF. In a mixing bowl, add the spinach, cream cheese, parmesan, black pepper, garlic salt, garlic paste, and parsley. Mix the ingredients until well combined to create the filler.

FOR THE SALMON

STEP 2. Rinse the salmon fillets with a mix of white vinegar and water, then pat them dry with a paper towel. Sprinkle Mrs. Dash onto both sides of each salmon fillet. Slice a pocket, lengthwise along the top of each fillet, right down the center. Stuff each fillet with filler (about a spoonful).

STEP 3. Warm a sauté pan over medium-high heat. Sear each fillet for 2-3 minutes on each side.

STEP 4. Place the salmon fillets in a baking dish then cover the dish with foil. Bake for 8-10 minutes. Remove the salmon from the oven, discard the foil then return the dish to the oven. Broil the salmon fillets for 2-4 minutes, or until golden brown. This Stuffed Salmon is delicious with rice and green beans.

STEAK & SHRIMP

FOR THE STEAK

- ½ teaspoon Minced Garlic
- 3 (8-ounce) Bone-In New York Strips
- ½ tablespoon Blackened Seasoning
- ¼ tablespoon Paprika, to taste
- ¼ tablespoon Black Pepper, to taste
- ½ teaspoon Dried Rosemary
- ¼ tablespoon Garlic powder
- 1 ½ teaspoon Butter
- Fresh Rosemary (optional)

FOR THE SHRIMP

- 1 tablespoon Minced Garlic
- 1 tablespoon Butter
- 1 lb Shrimp, peeled and deveined
- 1 teaspoon Old Bay Seasoning
- 1 tablespoon Fresh Parsley
- Fresh Cracked Pepper, to taste

TOTAL TIME 20-25 MINUTES

SERVES 4-6

FOR THE STEAK

STEP 1. Preheat the oven to 350ºF. Rub minced garlic over the top and bottom of each strip. Evenly sprinkle blackened seasoning, paprika, black pepper, dried rosemary, and garlic powder over all three steaks.

STEP 2. Place ½ teaspoon of butter on top of each steak. Grill the steak for 3-4 minutes on each side for a nice sear.

STEP 3. Place the steaks into the oven to finish. Allow the steak to cook to your preferred temperature before removing it. Example: Medium = firm pink center or 140ºF.

FOR THE SHRIMP

STEP 4. Warm a sauté pan over medium-high heat. Add the minced garlic, butter, and shrimp to the pan—season with Old Bay seasoning, and Parsley. Sauté for 5-8 minutes. Once both the steak and shrimp have fully cooked, serve together with a pinch of fresh cracked pepper.

NOTE: You can grill, bake, or pan sear the steaks to the preferred temperature.

BABY BACK RIBS

FOR THE RIBS

STEP 1. Preheat the oven to 425ºF. Wash the ribs with a mixture of white vinegar and water. Pull off the thin film from the back of the ribs. Pat dry. Coat both sides of the ribs with olive oil. Mix together the Dry Rub ingredients, setting aside 1/4 cup of the mixture if you plan to make the BBQ sauce. Evenly coat both sides of the ribs with the dry rub. Marinate in the refrigerator for 45 minutes to an hour, or overnight if you want more intense flavor.

STEP 2. Tightly wrap the ribs in a sheet of foil. Set the ribs bone side down on a baking sheet. Bake in the oven for 30-45 minutes on one side, flipping them to cook for 30-45 minutes on the other side.

FOR THE SAUCE

STEP 3. In a medium-sized pot, whisk together the BBQ sauce ingredients over medium heat. Reduce the heat to low and simmer for 15-20 minutes.

STEP 4. Take the ribs out of the oven and remove the foil. Fully coat the ribs in barbecue sauce on both sides, then return to the oven to broil for 5-10 minutes. Use a slicing knife to separate each rib before serving.

FOR THE RIBS

- Full rack of Baby Back Ribs
- 2 tablespoons Olive Oil

FOR DRY RUB

- 1 tablespoon Black Pepper
- 1 ½ tablespoon Seasoned Salt
- 1 tablespoon Paprika
- 1 tablespoon Onion Powder
- ½ tablespoon Blackened Seasoning
- ¼ cup of Brown Sugar
- ½ teaspoon Cayenne Pepper (optional)
- 2 tablespoons BBQ Sauce (or make your own)

FOR THE BBQ SAUCE

- ¾ cup Ketchup
- ⅛ cup Butter
- 1 tablespoon Worcestershire sauce
- 1 tablespoon Brown Spicy Mustard
- ⅓ cup Brown sugar
- ¼ cup Dry Rub
- ⅛ teaspoon Cayenne Pepper (optional)

TOTAL TIME 1.5 HOURS

SERVES 4-6

STUFFED TURKEY MEATLOAF

FOR THE SAUCE

- ½ cup Ketchup
- ½ cup BBQ Sauce

FOR THE MEATLOAF

- ½ cup White Onion
- 2 teaspoons Minced Garlic
- 6-pounds of Ground Turkey
- 2 Eggs, beaten
- 1 ½ tablespoon Onion Powder
- 1 ½ tablespoon Blackened Seasoning
- 1 ½ tablespoon Garlic Salt
- 1 cup of Breadcrumbs
- 1 tablespoon Olive Oil
- 1 cup Cheddar Cheese (or to preference)
- 1 teaspoon Paprika
- 2/3 tablespoons Parsley

COOK TIME 45 MINUTES

SERVING SIZE 8-12

STEP 1. Preheat the oven to 350ºF. Combine the ketchup and BBQ sauce in a small mixing bowl.

STEP 2. Sauté the onions and garlic in a sauté pan for 1-2 minutes.

STEP 3. Place the ground turkey into a mixing bowl, add the cooked onions, minced garlic, and the two beaten eggs. Using clean hands, mix the garlic, onions, and egg into the ground turkey. Season the ground turkey with onion powder, blackened seasoning, and garlic salt. Pour in the breadcrumbs. Mix well.

STEP 4. Use olive oil to grease the bottom of a baking pan. Place half of the ground turkey mixture onto the baking pan in the shape of a loaf. Place a layer of cheese in the center and then cover with the remaining ground turkey mixture. Shape the turkey loaf around the cheese, sealing it. Leave about a 1-inch space on each side of the baking pan.

STEP 5. Generously sprinkle paprika over the top and sides of the meatloaf. Cover the baking pan with foil and place the meatloaf in the oven for 15 minutes.

STEP 6. Remove the foil from the baking pan then allow the meatloaf to bake uncovered for about 20 minutes.

STEP 7. Using a silicone brush, generously spread the BBQ sauce and ketchup mixture over the meatloaf and garnish with parsley.

LOBSTER FRIED RICE

- 4 (4-ounce) Coldwater Lobster tails
- 2 tablespoons Butter
- 1 tablespoon Minced Garlic
- 1 tablespoon Parsley
- 1 tablespoon Cilantro
- ½ cup White Onions, diced
- ¾ cup Frozen Mixed Vegetables (green beans, corn, carrots, peas)
- Olive Oil, to coat the pan
- 2 Eggs
- 3 cups White Rice, cooked (chilled 12-24 hours)
- ¼ teaspoon Mrs. Dash
- 1 tablespoon Black Pepper
- 1 tablespoon Garlic Salt
- 1 tablespoon Hoisin
- 1 ½ tablespoon Soy Sauce

TOTAL TIME 35 MINUTES

SERVES 6

STEP 1. Cut open the lobster tails and remove the meat. Rinse the lobster with a mix of white vinegar and water.

STEP 2. Warm a wok over medium heat. Add butter, minced garlic, parsley, and cilantro. Toss in the lobster. Cook for 4-5 minutes, then remove the it from the wok. Set aside in a bowl.

STEP 3. Add the onion and frozen vegetables. Sauté until they have cooked through. Remove the vegetables from the wok.

STEP 4. Clean the wok then pour in the olive oil. Place the wok over medium-high heat. Crack the eggs into the wok and scramble them until they have cooked through. Remove the eggs from the pan and place in the same bowl as the lobster.

STEP 5. Add more olive oil to the wok and warm it over medium-high heat. Place the precooked white rice into the wok and then season with Mrs. Dash, black pepper, and garlic salt. Pour in hoisin sauce and soy sauce. Continue stir-frying and cooking the rice for 3-4 minutes.

STEP 6. Place the lobster, sautéed vegetables, and scrambled eggs back into the wok. Stir-fry the together before serving.

JAMBALAYA CREOLE RICE

- 2-pounds Shrimp
- 1 ½ - 2 lbs Chicken Breast, diced
- 3 cups Jasmine Rice
- 4 Andouille Sausages, sliced
- 2 tablespoons of Olive Oil
- ½ teaspoon Black Pepper
- 1 Red Bell Pepper, diced
- 1 Green Bell Pepper, diced
- 1 Yellow Bell Pepper, diced
- 1 Orange Bell Pepper, diced
- 3 Stalks Celery, diced
- 1 White Onion, diced
- 1 Chicken Bouillon Cube
- 1 Tomato Bouillon Cube
- 4 ½ cups Chicken Stock
- 1 cup Water
- ½ teaspoon Garlic Powder
- ½ teaspoon Onion Powder
- 1 teaspoon Paprika
- ½ teaspoon Old Bay Seasoning
- 1 teaspoon Cajun Seasoning
- ½ teaspoon Red Ground Pepper
- ½ teaspoon Cayenne Pepper
- 1 teaspoon Blackened Seasoning
- ½ teaspoon Chili Powder

TOTAL TIME 1 HOUR

SERVES 10-12

NOTE: Caution! This dish will be hot and spicy.

STEP 1. Rinse the shrimp and chicken with a mix of white vinegar and water. Using a colander thoroughly rinse the rice with water.

STEP 2. Sauté the sausage by itself first for 5-6 minutes over medium heat. Remove the sausage and set it aside in a bowl. Keep the fat residue inside the sauté pan.

STEP 3. Drizzle olive oil into the pan then toss in the chicken to cook by itself for 5-8 minutes. Remove the chicken and set it aside in the same bowl as the sausage. Keep the fat residue in the sauté pan.

STEP 4. Toss the shrimp into the sauté pan. Season with black pepper. Cook the shrimp by itself for 3-5 minutes. Remove the shrimp from the pan and set it aside in a separate bowl from the sausage and chicken. Keep the fat residue in the sauté pan.

STEP 5. Add the bell peppers, celery, and onions and sauté for 3 minutes. Add the chicken and tomato bouillon cubes. Pour in the rice, chicken stock and water, then stir well. Season the rice with garlic powder, onion powder, paprika, old bay, Cajun seasoning, red ground pepper, cayenne pepper, blackened seasoning, and chili powder. Simmer the rice over medium heat for 10-15 minutes.

STEP 6. After the rice has simmered for 10-15 minutes, stir in the chicken and sausage then cook for an additional 10 minutes. Lastly, mix in the shrimp and reduce the heat to low. Simmer for 10 minutes, then serve promptly, garnished with parsley and a lemon wedge.

PEPPERED STEAK

STEP 1. Slice the steak into strips then add them to a mixing bowl. Sprinkle in onion powder, garlic powder, black pepper, paprika, and blackened seasoning. Thoroughly toss the steak in the seasonings to fully coat.

STEP 2. Warm the butter in a sauté pan over medium heat. Sauté the steak for 6-8 minutes or until it has cooked to your preference.

STEP 3. Add rosemary, minced garlic, onions, mushrooms, and bell peppers. Sauté for 5 minutes.

STEP 4. Pour the beef stock into the pan along with the soy sauce and Worcestershire sauce. Simmer over low heat for 5 minutes. Serve promptly with a side of rice.

- 1-pound of Steak, sliced
- 1 teaspoon Onion Powder
- 1 teaspoon Garlic Powder
- 1 teaspoon Black Pepper
- ¼ tablespoon Paprika
- 1 teaspoon Blackened Seasoning
- 1 tablespoon Butter
- ½ tablespoon Fresh Rosemary, chopped
- 1 tablespoon Minced Garlic
- 1 White Onion, sliced
- 1 (8-ounce) can of Mushrooms
- 1 Red Bell Pepper, sliced
- 1 Green Bell Pepper, sliced
- 1 Yellow Bell Pepper, sliced
- 1 Orange Bell Pepper, sliced
- 2 cups Beef Stock
- 1 tablespoon Soy Sauce
- 1 tablespoon Worcestershire Sauce

TOTAL TIME 20 MINUTES
SERVES 2-4

NOTE: If you want thicker gravy, mix cornstarch and water in a separate bowl, then add it to the pan as needed.

FRIED CATFISH

- 4 (6-8 ounce) Catfish Fillets
- 1 teaspoon Old Bay Seasoning
- 1 teaspoon Blackened Seasoning
- 1 teaspoon Onion Powder
- ¼ teaspoon Black Pepper
- ¼ teaspoon Cajun Seasoning

FOR THE COATING

- 2 Eggs
- 1 teaspoon Water
- 1 cup of Cornmeal
- ½ cup Flour
- 1 teaspoon Cajun Seasoning
- 1 teaspoon Old Bay Seasoning
- 1 teaspoon Blackened Seasoning
- 4-6 cups Vegetable Oil

TOTAL TIME 15 MINUTES

SERVES 4

STEP 1. Rinse the catfish with a mix of white vinegar and water, pat dry with a paper towel. Season the catfish with Old Bay seasoning, blackened seasoning, onion powder, black pepper, and Cajun seasoning.

STEP 2. Crack the eggs into a mixing bowl, add a teaspoon of water then whisk.

STEP 3. In a separate bowl, add the cornmeal, flour, Cajun seasoning, Old Bay seasoning, and blackened seasoning. Whisk together to create the batter.

STEP 4. Preheat vegetable oil in a deep fryer or frying pan to 350ºF. The pan should be about half way full of oil. Coat the fish in the egg wash, then coat it in the batter on both sides. Drop the fish into the fryer or frying pan and cook for 3-5 minutes or until golden-brown. Remove the fish from the oil. Drain off the excess oil using a cooling rack before serving. Serve with lemon wedge.

THE KITCHEN IS A PLACE TO EXPERIENCE HAPPY VIBES, MAKE GREAT MEMORIES AND BOND WITH LOVED ONES.

SEAFOOD BOIL

STEP 1. Rinse the shrimp with a mix of white vinegar and water. Bring 7 quarts of water to a boil in a stockpot. Toss in the crawfish boil bag, onion, lemon, thyme, and garlic. Boil for 5 minutes.

STEP 2. Add the potatoes and boil until they have softened, about 7-10 minutes. Remove the potatoes then place them in a bowl.

STEP 3. Add the shrimp, crab legs, and corn, to the stockpot. Boil for 5 minutes, then remove and place the corn, crab legs, and shrimp in the same bowl that you placed the potatoes into.

STEP 4. Begin making the sauce in a saucepan by adding two sticks of butter along with garlic and onions. Pour in a cup of water from the seafood boil. Add all of the "for the sauce" seasonings. Simmer the sauce over medium heat for 15-20 minutes while stirring occasionally.

STEP 5. Pour the sauce over the seafood boil, then serve.

NOTE: When adding water to the sauce, use water from the seafood boil or it will lack flavor. If you prefer a thicker sauce, mix one-part cornstarch and two-parts water in a bowl, and pour it into the sauce as needed to achieve the thickness you prefer.

FOR THE SEAFOOD

- 2 ½-pounds Shrimp
- 7 Quarts Water
- 1 Crawfish Boil Bag
- ½ of a White Onion, chopped
- 1 ½ Lemons, sliced
- 3 sprigs Thyme
- 10 Garlic Cloves
- 2-pounds Red Potatoes
- 6-pounds Jumbo King Crab Legs
- 12 Frozen Corn Mini Ears

FOR THE SAUCE

- 2 sticks Butter
- ½ tablespoon Minced Garlic
- ½ cup Onion
- 1 cup Water (from the seafood boil)
- ½ tablespoon Cumin
- 2 teaspoons Paprika
- ½ tablespoon Chili Powder
- ½ teaspoon Crushed Red Pepper
- ½ tablespoon Cajun seasoning
- ½ tablespoon Lemon Pepper Seasoning
- ½ tablespoon Ground Pepper
- ½ tablespoon Black Pepper
- ½ tablespoon Onion Powder
- ½ tablespoon Italian Seasoning
- 1 tablespoon Worcestershire Sauce
- 1 tablespoon Hot Chili Oil
- ½ tablespoon Blackened Seasoning
- 1 tablespoon Spicy Chili Crisp
- 1 Chicken Bouillon Cube
- 1 Tomato Bouillon Cube

TOTAL TIME 30 MINUTES
SERVES 6

Island
TINGZ

CURRY CHICKEN

- 4-6 Chicken Drumsticks (or any cut of chicken)
- 2 tablespoons All-Purpose Poultry Seasoning
- 1 teaspoon Black pepper
- 1 tablespoon Garlic Salt
- 1 teaspoon Garlic Powder
- ½ Green Bell Pepper, chopped
- ½ Red Bell Pepper, chopped
- 1 Scotch Bonnet
- 1 Scallion (Green Onion)
- 1 tablespoon Minced Garlic
- 3 sprigs Fresh Thyme
- 3 tablespoons Olive Oil
- 1 tablespoon Curry Powder
- 1 ½ cup Water
- 1 tablespoon Pimentos/All Spice
- 1 Chicken Bouillon Cube

TOTAL TIME 30 MINUTES
SERVES 5-6

NOTE: Cut open the scotch bonnet and remove its seeds, unless you like extra spice! Curry powder will stain so be cautious when handling this ingredient. Curry powder can also upset the stomach, so you must toast it first. In the islands, we say "burn the spice!"

STEP 1. Begin by removing all of the skin from the chicken. Chop off the bottom ends of the drumsticks with a meat cleaver and then discard the trimmings. Rinse the chicken with a mix of white vinegar and water. Drain all of the water off then pat dry using a paper towel. (You want the chicken to be dry so it can hold the seasonings).

STEP 2. Place the chicken in a mixing bowl. Season with poultry seasoning, black pepper, garlic salt, garlic powder, bell peppers, scotch bonnet, green onions, garlic and thyme. Mix thoroughly to completely coat the chicken.

STEP 3. In a large Dutch pot heat three tablespoons of olive oil. Burn (toast) the curry powder in olive oil.

STEP 4. Remove only the chicken from the mixing bowl (leaving the vegetables) place in the Dutch pot. Cook the chicken for 3-4 minutes on each side for a nice golden-brown sear (increase the cook time for thicker chicken).

STEP 5. After browning the chicken, remove it from the Dutch pot and set it aside. Leave the drippings in the pot. Add the vegetables to the pot. Pour in the water followed by the pimento to create the gravy.

STEP 6. Place the chicken back in the pot with a chicken bouillon cube. Simmer for 25 minutes or until the gravy thickens, and the chicken is tender.

STEP 7. Check the chicken to make sure it has cooked completely. Serve with Jasmine Rice (Next Recipe).

JASMINE RICE

- 6 cups Rice
- 6 ½ cups Water
- 3 tablespoons Butter (unsalted)
- 4 sprigs of Fresh Thyme

TOTAL TIME 30 MINUTES

SERVES 6-10

STEP 1. Pour the jasmine rice into a large pot. Rinse the rice by filling a large pot with water then draining it. Rinse until the water runs clear.

STEP 2. Fill a large pot with 6 ½ cups of water, add butter, thyme and Italian seasoning. Cover the rice and simmer over medium-low heat for about 15 - 20 minutes.

STEP 3. Remove the lid when all water has evaporated and rice looks fluffy. Serve immediately.

NOTE: For every cup of white rice use one cup of water. If you do not have fresh Thyme, replace with 1/2 tablespoon of Italian Seasoning.

HOME-COOKED MEALS CAN BE EASY, FUN, AND VERY REWARDING.

CURRY SHRIMP

- 2 pounds Shrimp (41-60ct)
- 1 teaspoon Garlic Powder
- 1 tablespoon Minced Garlic
- 1 tablespoon All Purpose Seasoning
- 1 teaspoon Pimento Seeds/All Spice Berries
- 2 teaspoons Parsley
- 2 tablespoons Old Bay Seasoning
- ¾ cup of Tri-colored Bell Peppers, chopped
- 1 Scotch Bonnet
- 3 tablespoons Olive Oil
- 1 tablespoon Curry Powder
- ½ cup Coconut Milk
- ½ cup Water

TOTAL TIME 20 MINUTES
SERVES 5-6

STEP 1. Peel and devein the shrimp then rinse with a mix of water and white vinegar. In a mixing bowl, season the shrimp with garlic powder, minced garlic, All Purpose Seasoning, Pimento Seeds, Parsley, and Old Bay seasoning. Add the bell peppers and scotch bonnet. Mix the ingredients until thoroughly combined.

STEP 2. Heat the olive oil in a skillet then burn (toast) the curry powder. Add the shrimp to the skillet, stir to coat shrimp completely in the curry. Cook for 5-7 minutes.

STEP 3. Pour in the coconut milk and water, stir then cook for 1-2 minutes. The mixture will thicken and transform into a gravy.

STEP 4. Allow the shrimp to simmer in the gravy for 10-15 minutes on low-medium heat before serving with jasmine rice.

RICE & PEAS

- 10 cups Water
- 1-pound of Red Kidney Beans (Peas)
- 3 tablespoons Butter
- 1 (13.5-ounce) can Coconut Milk
- 1 Scotch Bonnet
- 3 sprigs Thyme
- 1/4 teaspoon All-Purpose Seasoning
- ¼ teaspoon Black Pepper
- ⅛ teaspoon Garlic Salt
- ¼ teaspoon Garlic Powder
- Chicken, Beef, Or Vegetable Bouillon Cube (optional)
- 1 tablespoon Pimento Seeds/All Spice Berries
- 3 cups Jasmine Rice
- 1 Plastic Bag

TOTAL TIME 1 HOUR SERVES 12-14

STEP 1. Begin by boiling 10 cups of water in a large pot. Next, pour in the peas. Cook the peas for 30 minutes until they are semi-soft.

STEP 2. Add butter, coconut milk, a scotch bonnet, and thyme to the pot then stir the ingredients. Season the peas with all-purpose seasoning, black pepper, garlic salt, garlic powder, and the optional bouillon cube Add the pimento seeds. Stir well. Cover the pot and cook for 5-8 minutes.

STEP 3. Rinse the rice in a large bowl or colander and then add it to the pot. Cover the pot with a plastic bag then place a lid over the bag.

STEP 4. Allow the rice and peas to steam on low heat for roughly 30 minutes. Remove the plastic bag. Serve the rice and peas immediately.

NOTE: Let the rice and peas steam, DO NOT stir.

Rice & Peas is a prominent Jamaican side dish. The dish is Jamaican slang, but in American terms, it is merely white rice and red kidney beans. It is the perfect side dish for oxtails.

The plastic bag makes the perfect rice (special trick). I like to use a plastic grocery bag. Cut the bag in half, then use the side without any dye on it. Wash it with soap and water before placing it over the rice.

JAMAICAN CABBAGE

- 1 stalk Broccoli, chopped or Bag of Fresh Broccoli
- 1 head Cabbage, chopped
- ½ tablespoon Olive Oil
- 2 tablespoons Water, separated
- 1 tablespoon Minced Garlic
- ¼ cup Red Onions, sliced
- 1 bag (10-ounce) Shredded Carrots
- 1 teaspoon Garlic Salt
- 1 tablespoon All-Purpose Seasoning
- 1 teaspoon Black Pepper
- ¼ teaspoon Crushed Red Pepper (optional)

TOTAL TIME: 20 MINUTES

SERVING SIZE: 6-8

STEP 1. Begin by chopping the stalk of broccoli into bite-sized pieces, then rinse. Drain the excess water and set aside. Repeat this for the head of cabbage and set aside, separately.

STEP 2. Add olive oil to a pan and sauté the minced garlic. Add the cabbage to the pot. Cover and let steam for 5 minutes, adding 1 tablespoon of water.

STEP 3. Remove the lid and add the broccoli, red onions, carrots, garlic salt, all-purpose seasoning, black pepper and red crushed pepper (optional). Stir, cover, and let steam for 3-4 minutes.

STEP 4. Uncover, adding another tablespoon of water and let steam for another 5-8 minutes. Cabbage should then be done. I love this dish served with Curry Chicken or Oxtails!

RASTA PASTA

FOR THE SHRIMP
- 2 pounds Shrimp
- 1 Green Bell Pepper, sliced
- 1 Red Bell Pepper, sliced
- 1 Yellow Bell Pepper, sliced
- ½ tablespoon Minced Garlic
- 2 teaspoons Parsley
- ¼ teaspoon Black Pepper
- 1 tablespoon Jerk Seasoning (Walkerswood, recommended)
- 1 teaspoon Old Bay Seasoning
- ½ cup Green Onions/Scallions, chopped
- 3 tablespoons Olive Oil

FOR THE SAUCE
- 3 Garlic Cloves
- 4 cups Heavy Whipping Cream
- ½ teaspoon Garlic Salt
- ½ teaspoon Onion Powder
- 1 teaspoon Cumin
- 1 teaspoon Paprika
- 3 sprigs Thyme
- ½ teaspoon Cajun seasoning (optional)
- ¾ cup Mozzarella Cheese, shredded
- ¾ cup Parmesan Cheese, shredded
- ¾ cup Italian Cheese Blend

FOR THE PASTA
- 2 lb. box Penne Pasta
- ½ teaspoon Parsley
- ½ teaspoon Cilantro
- ½ teaspoon Butter
- pinch of Himalayan Pink Salt

TOTAL TIME 45 MINUTES

SERVES 8-10

FOR THE SHRIMP

STEP 1. Start by rinsing the shrimp with a mix of white vinegar and water. In a mixing bowl, season the shrimp by adding minced garlic, parsley, old bay, black pepper, and jerk seasoning. Mix and set aside.

STEP 2. Slice the bell peppers into thin slices. Chop the garlic cloves and green onions.

STEP 3. In a large sauce pan, add 1 tablespoon of olive oil and shrimp. Sautee the shrimp for 5-7 minutes. Remove shrimp from pot and set aside. Add to the pot 1 tablespoon olive oil, minced garlic, bell peppers, parsley, onions, and thyme. Cover and let cook for 5-7 minutes.

FOR THE SAUCE

STEP 4. After letting the bell pepper cook for 5-7 minutes, pour in the heavy whipping cream. Sprinkle in garlic salt, onion powder, cumin, paprika, and Cajun seasoning for flavor. Stir well.

STEP 5. After the sauce has warmed to a slight boil, add all of the cheeses. Continue to simmer and stir the sauce until it reaches a nice and creamy consistency. Turn off the heat.

FOR THE PASTA

STEP 6. In a medium-sized pot, bring water to a boil. Toss in the penne noodles, and a pinch of Himalayan salt. Boil the penne noodles to al dente or still slightly firm in texture. Drain the penne noodles.

STEP 7. After you have drained the pasta, add butter and garlic salt, then stir. Add pasta and shrimp to the sauté pan, then mix ingredients thoroughly. Cover the pan with a lid.

STEP 8. Simmer the pasta on low-medium heat for around 5-8 minutes. Try this Rasta Pasta with a Sip After Dark recipe, I recommend the "Drunk Text!"

NOTE: If you want extra spice, add more Cajun seasoning but be mindful that the jerk seasoning has a kick! I suggest that you taste the dish before adding more spice. Coconut milk can be used as a substitute for heavy whipping cream, and chicken is a great alternative for the shrimp.

OXTAIL

- 3-pounds Oxtail
- 1 Green Bell Pepper, diced (optional)
- ¼ cup Scallions/Green Onions, chopped
- ½ of a White Onion, medium sliced (optional)
- 3 cloves of Garlic, chopped
- 3 sprigs Thyme
- 1 Scotch Bonnet (make sure the seeds are removed)
- 1 teaspoon Pimentos/All Spice Berries
- ½ tablespoon Seasoned Salt (Lawry's recommended)
- ⅙ teaspoon Cayenne pepper
- ½ tablespoon Oxtail seasoning (Grace recommended)
- ½ tablespoon Onion powder
- Black Pepper, to taste
- 1 tablespoon Worcestershire Sauce
- 1 tablespoon Soy sauce
- 1 tablespoon Browning sauce (Grace recommended)
- 5 tablespoons of Olive Oil
- 1-2 cups Water
- 1 Beef Bouillon Cube (optional)
- 1 (16-ounce) can of Butter Beans (No Lima Beans)
- 1 tablespoon Ketchup

COOK TIME 2-3 HOURS

SERVING SIZE 8-10

STEP 1. Rinse the oxtails with a mix of water and white vinegar, then place them into a large mixing bowl.

STEP 2. Add the bell pepper, green onion, white onion, garlic, thyme, scotch bonnet, pimentos, seasoned salt, cayenne pepper, oxtail seasoning, onion powder, and black pepper. Next, pour in the Worcestershire sauce, soy sauce, and browning sauce. Using clean hands, toss the mixture to combine the ingredients thoroughly.

STEP 3. Warm the olive oil in a large Dutch pot over medium-high heat.

STEP 4. Remove only the oxtails (not vegetables) from the mixing bowl then place them in the Dutch pot. Set vegetables aside. Brown the oxtails on each side for 5-8 minutes depending on thickness (Thicker oxtails will need to be cooked longer).

STEP 5. Gently pour in water until the oxtails are halfway covered. Lower the heat to medium and cover the pot. Cook for 2-3 hours, minimum. The water will start to thicken into a gravy. Check the oxtails every 30-45 minutes. The oxtails should remain halfway covered with water, add more as necessary. Be careful not to add too much water, the oxtail gravy should not be thin like soup. (This is key to the process.)

STEP 6. Once the oxtails have cooked halfway or for 1 ½ -2 hours, add the beef bouillon cube. Toss in the vegetable mixture: bell peppers, green onion, white onion, garlic, thyme, and a scotch bonnet. Stir to combine.

STEP 7. Stir in the butter beans and ketchup, cover the pot, and cook for another hour.

STEP 8. Simmer until the oxtails are fork tender, and the gravy thickens to your preference. Once they are done, serve with rice and peas!

NOTE: The brands that I recommend will give the dish authentic Jamaican flavor.

BROWN STEW CHICKEN

- 4-pounds Chicken Legs or Thighs
- 2 tablespoons Browning Sauce (Grace recommended)
- 1 tablespoon All-Purpose Seasoning
- 1 tablespoon Onion Powder
- 1 tablespoon Garlic Salt
- ½ tablespoon Black Pepper
- 1 tablespoon Fresh Garlic minced
- ½ of a Green Bell Pepper, diced
- ½ of an Orange Bell Pepper, diced
- 2 Carrots, chopped
- 1 ½ tablespoon Scallions/Green Onions
- 3 sprigs Thyme
- 2 tablespoons Olive Oil
- 3 Russet Potatoes peeled & chopped
- 1 Chicken Bouillon Cube
- 1 Scotch Bonnet
- 1 tablespoon Ketchup

COOK TIME 35-40 MINUTES

SERVING SIZE 6-8

STEP 1. Remove the skin from the chicken before you begin. If using chicken legs, chop off the bottom joint of the chicken legs using a meat cleaver. Rinse the chicken with a mix of white vinegar and water, pat dry with a paper towel, and then place it into a mixing bowl.

STEP 2. Pour the browning sauce into the mixing bowl along with the all-purpose seasoning, onion powder, garlic salt, black pepper, minced garlic, bell peppers, carrots, green onions, and thyme. Mix to thoroughly coat the chicken with seasonings and vegetables.

STEP 3. Warm the olive oil in a Dutch pot over medium heat. Add the chicken alone without the vegetables, and then brown for 5-7 minutes on each side.

STEP 4. Add the potatoes, chicken bouillon cube, scotch bonnet and vegetables to the pot with the chicken. Stir to combine. Mix in the ketchup, then fill the pot about halfway with water. Cover and simmer for about 30 minutes or until the chicken is cooked through.

JERK CORNISH HENS

- 2 Cornish Hens
- ½ of White Onion, diced
- 2 tablespoons Butter, divided (to stuff in hens)
- 2 Chicken Bouillon Cubes
- 4 sprigs of Thyme
- 1 teaspoon Butter, melted
- 1 tablespoon Poultry Seasoning (1/2 on each hen)
- ¼ teaspoon Garlic Powder
- ¼ teaspoon Black Pepper
- ¼ teaspoon Garlic Salt
- ¼ teaspoon Onion Powder
- 4 tablespoons Jerk Seasoning
- Cilantro or Parsley, to taste
- 2 teaspoons Chicken Stock (optional)

COOK TIME 45 MINUTES
SERVING SIZE 6-8

STEP 1. Preheat the oven to 400ºF. Begin by cutting off the neck and tail of each hen. Rinse the hens with a mix of white vinegar and water, pat dry with a paper towel.

STEP 2. Place the hens in a baking pan. Stuff each hen with the white onion, butter, one bouillon cube, and 2 sprigs of thyme. Pour the melted butter over each Cornish hen then season each side evenly with poultry seasoning, garlic powder, black pepper, garlic salt, and onion powder. Give them that extra boost of Caribbean flavor by rubbing jerk seasoning all over!

STEP 3. Sprinkle cilantro or parsley over the hens.

STEP 4. Cover the baking pan with foil. (You can pour a little chicken stock in for extra juiciness). Bake the Cornish hens for 30-45 minutes.

STEP 5. Uncover the baking pan, then broil the hens for 5-8 minute before serving.

JERK SALMON

FOR THE SALMON

- 2-pound fillet Salmon
- 1 tablespoon Jerk Seasoning Dry Rub
- 1 teaspoon Minced Garlic Butter (if you prefer to bake)
- 1 teaspoon Olive Oil

FOR THE BBQ SAUCE

- ¾ cup Ketchup
- ⅛ cup Butter
- 1 tablespoon Worcestershire sauce
- 1 tablespoon Brown Spicy Mustard
- ⅓ cup Brown sugar
- ¼ cup Jerk Seasoning
- ⅛ teaspoon Cayenne Pepper (Optional for more spice)

TOTAL TIME 15 MINUTES

SERVES 4-6

FOR THE SALMON

STEP 1. Rinse the salmon with a mix of white vinegar and water. Pat the salmon dry with a paper towel to remove the excess water.

STEP 2. Rub the bottom of the salmon with olive oil. Evenly season the entire filet with the dry rub jerk seasoning and minced garlic.

FOR THE BBQ SAUCE

STEP 3. In a small saucepan over medium-low heat, whisk together the BBQ sauce ingredients. Simmer for 15-20 minutes then remove from heat.

STEP 4. Pan sear the salmon, flesh side down, over high heat for 5-6 minutes on each side. Alternatively, place the salmon in a casserole dish and top with a teaspoon of butter then cover with foil. Place it in the oven and bake at 400ºF for 12-15 minutes. Remove from oven when completed, then spread BBQ sauce over salmon.

Cookin'
UP A BIRD

SESAME CHICKEN

FOR THE CHICKEN

- 1 ½ pounds of Boneless Chicken Breast
- ⅛ teaspoon of Black pepper
- ½ teaspoon of Garlic salt
- ⅛ teaspoon of Ground White Pepper
- ¾ cup Flour
- ¼ cup Cornstarch
- ¼ teaspoon Baking Powder
- 1 Egg White
- ¾ cups Water
- 4-6 cups Vegetable Oil

FOR THE SESAME SAUCE

- ¼ cup of Brown Sugar
- 1 tablespoon Sesame oil
- 1 ½ teaspoons Rice vinegar
- 1 teaspoon of Honey
- 1 teaspoon of Sriracha sauce
- 1 teaspoon of Soy sauce
- ⅛ teaspoon of Garlic salt
- ½ teaspoon of Hoisin sauce
- ½ teaspoon of Water
- Sesame Seeds, to preference

TOTAL TIME 30 MINUTES

SERVES 6

FOR THE CHICKEN

STEP 1. Rinse the chicken breast with a mixture of white vinegar and water then dice the chicken into 1- inch cubes. Season with black pepper, garlic salt, and ground white pepper.

STEP 2. To create the batter, combine the flour, cornstarch, baking powder, and an egg white in a mixing bowl. Whisk the ingredients while gradually adding water to the mixture.

STEP 3. Preheat vegetable oil in the frying pan or deep fryer to 350ºF. Dip the diced chicken into the batter until fully coated, shake off any excess. Place the battered chicken into the hot oil then fry to golden brown, about 3-5 minutes. Strain the chicken on a wire rack.

FOR THE SESAME SAUCE

STEP 4. Place a saucepan over medium-high heat. In the saucepan, add brown sugar, sesame oil, rice vinegar, honey, Sriracha sauce, soy sauce, garlic salt, hoisin sauce, and water. Mix well. Simmer for 5 minutes then stir in the sesame seeds. Turn off the heat.

STEP 5. In a mixing bowl, toss the chicken in the sesame sauce until thoroughly coated then serve.

PAN SEARED CHICKEN

STEP 1. Rinse the chicken with a mix of white vinegar and water, pat dry with a paper towel. Season the chicken with salt, black pepper, garlic powder, paprika, and cayenne pepper.

STEP 2. Warm a pan over medium heat. Sear the chicken for 5-7 minutes on each side. Remove the chicken from the pan and set it aside. Leave the drippings in the pan.

STEP 3. Add the chicken stock to the pan. Whisk the chicken stock and flour into the pan drippings until the mixture is smooth.

STEP 4. Arrange the chicken onto a serving plate. Pour the sauce over the cooked chicken before serving. Garnish with fresh rosemary.

- 2-pounds Chicken Breast
- 1 ½ tablespoon Salt
- 1 ½ tablespoon Black pepper
- 1 tablespoon Garlic Powder
- 1 tablespoon Paprika
- 1 tablespoon Cayenne Pepper
- 1 cup Chicken Stock
- 1 ½ tablespoon Flour
- Fresh Rosemary Chopped

TOTAL TIME 25 MINUTES

SERVES 4

I DEVELOPED A LOVE AND PASSION FOR COOKING IN MY GRANDMOTHER'S KITCHEN.

FRIED CHICKEN

- 6 Eggs (5 egg whites & 1 whole egg)
- 1 teaspoon Honey
- 6 Chicken Legs or Thighs)
- 1 teaspoon Hot Sauce
- 1 teaspoon Cajun seasoning
- ½ teaspoon Onion powder
- ½ teaspoon Garlic Powder
- ⅛ teaspoon Garlic Salt
- ½ teaspoon Black Pepper
- 1 teaspoon Parsley Flakes
- 4-6 cups Vegetable Oil

FOR THE FLOUR MIX

- 1 Ziploc bag
- 3 cups Flour
- ½ cup of Baking Powder
- 1 tablespoon Cajun seasoning
- ¼ teaspoon Garlic salt
- ¼ teaspoon Garlic powder
- 1 teaspoon Onion Powder

TOTAL TIME 30 MINUTES

SERVES 6

STEP 1. After rinsing the chicken with a mix of white vinegar and water, remove the skin.

STEP 2. Add five egg whites and one whole egg to a mixing bowl. Stir in the honey (optional to make crust sweet). Whisk until the egg and honey mixture is completely combined.

STEP 3. Add the chicken to the mixing bowl then add hot sauce, Cajun seasoning, onion powder, garlic powder, garlic salt, black pepper, and parsley flakes. Mix well.

STEP 4. Make the flour mixture by placing the flour and baking powder inside a Ziplock bag. Add the Cajun seasoning, garlic salt, garlic powder, and onion powder.

STEP 5. Preheat vegetable oil to 350ºF in a frying pan or deep fryer. Dip the chicken in the egg white mixture until fully submerged. Next, toss the chicken into the Ziplock bag. Gently shake the bag to ensure the chicken is fully coated with flour. (Repeat for extra crispy chicken)

STEP 6. Submerge the chicken in the oil and fry for 10- 12 minutes. Flip the chicken halfway though.

STEP 7. Remove and place the chicken on a wire rack to drain excess oil. Serve hot.

SMOTHERED CHICKEN

- 1 Ziploc Bag
- 1 cup Vegetable Oil

FOR THE CHICKEN

- 6-8 Count Chicken thighs
- ½ tablespoon Old Bay Seasoning
- 1 teaspoon Onion Powder
- ½ teaspoon Garlic Salt
- ½ tablespoon Mrs. Dash
- ½ teaspoon Black Pepper
- ½ teaspoon Basil
- ½ teaspoon Paprika
- 1 teaspoon Cajun Seasoning

FOR THE FLOUR MIX

- ½ cup of Cornstarch
- 3 cups Flour
- ¼ teaspoon Garlic powder
- ¼ teaspoon Garlic Salt
- 1 teaspoon Onion Powder
- 1 tablespoon Cajun Seasoning

FOR THE GRAVY

- ½ White Onion, sliced
- ½ cup of Flour Mix
- ¼ teaspoon Crushed Red Pepper (optional)
- ½ tablespoon Minced Garlic
- 1 tablespoon Parsley
- 1 tablespoon Butter
- 2 cups Chicken Stock
- 1 cup of Heavy Cream

TOTAL TIME 45 MINUTES

SERVES 4-6

FOR THE CHICKEN

STEP 1. Preheat the oven to 375ºF. Rinse the chicken with a mixture of white vinegar and water. Pat the chicken dry with a paper towel. Place into a mixing bowl, then season the chicken with Old Bay, onion powder, garlic salt, Mrs. Dash, black pepper, basil, paprika, and Cajun seasoning. Mix well.

FOR THE FLOUR MIX

STEP 2. Prepare the Ziplock bag by folding it downward about halfway. Add the cornstarch and flour to the bag first. Next, add garlic powder, garlic salt, onion powder, and Cajun seasoning. Fold the Ziplock bag back up and seal it. Shake the bag to mix the seasonings. Unseal the bag then add a few chicken thighs. Shake the bag again to coat the chicken with the flour mix. Once you've coated all the chicken, DO NOT dispose of the flour mix. It will be used to make the gravy.

STEP 3. Fry the chicken in a cast iron skillet or an oven-safe frying pan for 4-5 minutes on each side, or until golden brown and the juices run clear. Remove the chicken and set it aside to drain on a wire rack. Pour the used oil from inside the pan into a separate bowl. Do not wash the pan! The fond will be used for the gravy.

FOR THE GRAVY

STEP 4. Take ½ a cup of the used oil and pour it back into the cast iron skillet. Toss in the white onions and sauté them for 1-2 minutes.

STEP 5. Add the remaining flour mix, crushed red pepper, minced garlic, parsley, and butter. Stir and cook for 5-8 minutes. The mixture should begin to bubble. Keep stirring until there are almost no bubbles.

STEP 6. Pour the chicken stock and heavy cream in the cast iron, then continue to stir for 3-4 minutes.

STEP 7. Use tongs to submerge the chicken into the gravy and coat it on all sides. Cover the cast iron skillet with foil then place it in the oven to bake for 30-35 minutes. Use an oven mitt to take the pan out the oven.

NOTE: You will need an oven-safe pan because you will be frying and baking in the same pan.

TUSCAN CHICKEN

FOR THE CHICKEN

- 1 teaspoon Garlic Powder
- 1 teaspoon Onion Powder
- 1 teaspoon Mrs. Dash
- 1 teaspoon Black Pepper
- ½ teaspoon Butter
- 4 Chicken Breasts

FOR THE SAUCE

- 2 cups Heavy Whipping Cream
- 1 tablespoon Butter
- 2 ½ cups Spinach
- 2/3 cup Sundried Tomatoes
- ½ teaspoon Onion Powder
- ⅛ cup Garlic Salt
- ¼ teaspoon Garlic Powder
- ¼ teaspoon Ground White Pepper
- 1 cup Parmesan Cheese

TOTAL TIME 20 MINUTES

SERVES 4

FOR THE CHICKEN

STEP 1. Rinse the chicken breasts with a mixture of white vinegar and water, pat dry. Season with garlic powder, onion powder, Mrs. Dash, and black pepper.

STEP 2. Toss the butter into a sauté pan over medium heat. Sear the chicken breasts for 3-4 on each side.

FOR THE SAUCE

STEP 3. Pour heavy cream in a saucepan pan over medium heat. Add the butter, spinach, and sundried tomatoes. Season the sauce with onion powder, garlic salt, garlic powder, and white pepper. Sprinkle in the parmesan. Whisk vigorously then cook until the sauce is creamy, about 5 minutes.

STEP 4. Add the chicken breast to the pan with the sauce and simmer over medium heat for at least 8 more minutes.

STEP 5. Cut into the middle of the chicken to check that it is cooked thoroughly. When serving, plate the chicken and smother with a generous amount of gravy.

STUFFED CHICKEN

STEP 1. Begin by preheating the oven to 350ºF.

FOR THE FILLING

STEP 2. In a mixing bowl, add the cheddar cheese and cream cheese. Use a spoon to break up the cream cheese a bit. Next include the minced garlic, ranch seasoning, Worcestershire sauce, hot sauce, parsley, black pepper, Italian seasoning, onion powder, and garlic powder. Use the back of the spoon to mash the ingredients together then stir until well combined.

FOR THE CHICKEN

STEP 3. Rinse the chicken with white vinegar and water. Slice an opening down the side of each chicken breast, lengthwise. Stuff one tablespoon of filling into each chicken breast. Stick three toothpicks in the chicken, one through the middle, and one through each end. Season the chicken with Mrs. Dash, paprika, and Italian seasoning.

STEP 4. Oil the bottom of the baking pan with butter or nonstick spray then place ½ tablespoon of butter on top of each chicken breast. Cover with aluminum foil, sealing each corner. Bake for at least 30 minutes. Check the center of the chicken to ensure it is cooked thoroughly. Thicker cuts of chicken will need to cook longer. After removing the chicken from the oven, allow it to rest for 6-8 minutes before serving. This will give the juices time to settle, increasing the flavor.

FOR THE FILLING

- 1 ½ cup of Sharp Cheddar Cheese, grated
- 1 (8-ounce) packet Cream Cheese
- 1 teaspoon Minced Garlic
- 1 ½ tablespoon Ranch Seasoning
- 1 tablespoon Worcestershire Sauce
- ¼ teaspoon Hot Sauce (optional)
- 1 tablespoon Parsley
- ¼ teaspoon Black Pepper
- 1 teaspoon Italian Seasoning
- ¼ teaspoon Onion Powder
- ¼ teaspoon Garlic Powder

FOR THE CHICKEN

- 2-pounds Chicken Breast, boneless, skinless
- Toothpicks
- ½ teaspoon Mrs. Dash
- ¼ teaspoon Paprika
- 1 teaspoon Italian Seasoning
- 2 tablespoons + ½ teaspoon Butter, divided

COOK TIME 30-35 MINUTES

SERVING SIZE 4-6

CHICKEN AND CHEESE ENCHILADAS

FOR THE ENCHILADA SAUCE

- 1 bag of Dried Red Chili Peppers (Remove all the seeds)
- 2 cups Water
- ½ of a White Onion, chopped
- 4 cloves of Garlic
- 1 Chicken Bouillon Cube
- ¼ teaspoon Cumin
- ¼ teaspoon Black Pepper
- ¼ teaspoon Oregano
- ¼ teaspoon Chili Powder

FOR THE ENCHILADAS

- 2 Chicken Breasts, diced
- ½ cup of Salsa Verde
- ½ teaspoon Onion Powder
- ½ teaspoon Garlic Powder
- ½ teaspoon Cumin
- ½ teaspoon Black Pepper
- ⅛ teaspoon Paprika
- Olive Oil, to coat the pan
- Shredded Cheese, to taste
- Corn or Flour Tortillas
- Taco Sauce, to taste

TOTAL TIME 40 MINUTES

SERVES 2

FOR THE ENCHILADA SAUCE

STEP 1. Preheat the oven to 400ºF. Roast the dried red chili peppers in a cast iron skillet over medium heat for 1-2 minutes. Boil the chili peppers in water for 10 minutes along with the chopped white onion, garlic, and bouillon cube. Save 2 – 3 cups of the boiled water, discard the rest.

STEP 2. Use a blender to purée the chili peppers, onions, garlic and the boiled water.

STEP 3. Strain the purée into a saucepan using a strainer. Stir the purée while it's in the strainer to help the enchilada sauce drip into the saucepan.

STEP 4. Season with cumin, black pepper, oregano, and chili powder, then stir. Allow the sauce to simmer 25-30 minutes on low heat.

FOR THE ENCHILADAS

STEP 5. Rinse the chicken with a mixture of white vinegar and water, pat dry with a paper towel. Dice the chicken breast into small pieces.

STEP 6. In a mixing bowl, season the chicken with Salsa Verde, onion powder, garlic powder, cumin, black pepper, and paprika. Toss the chicken in the seasonings.

STEP 7. Heat olive oil in the skillet and sauté the chicken for 10-12 minutes or until well done.

STEP 8. Lay the tortillas on a flat surface. Place an equal portion of the chicken inside each of the tortillas. Sprinkle shredded cheese on top. Roll the tortillas into an enchilada by folding one end over the other. Place the tortillas folded side down into the baking dish.

STEP 9. Drizzle the sauce over the enchiladas; sprinkle more shredded cheese over top. Place into the oven to bake for 15-20 minutes. Rest for 10 minutes before serving.

WET BURRITO

STEP 1. Rinse the chicken with a mixture of white vinegar and water, then pat dry with a paper towel. Dice the chicken breast.

STEP 2. Place the chicken into a mixing bowl along with the Salsa Verde, onion powder, garlic powder, cumin, black pepper, and paprika. Toss the chicken in the seasonings.

STEP 3. Heat the olive oil in a skillet over medium and sauté the chicken for 10-12 minutes or until it is well done.

STEP 4. Wrap the chicken, Mexican Rice and Beans (see Mexican Rice & Beans recipe) and cheese inside of the tortillas. Place the burritos in the baking dish.

STEP 5. Drizzle taco sauce or enchilada sauce over the burrito, then sprinkle more shredded cheese over the top. Place it in the oven to bake for 15-20 minutes. Serve hot with sour cream and cilantro to garnish.

- 2 Chicken Breasts
- ½ cup of Salsa Verde
- ½ teaspoon Onion Powder
- ½ teaspoon Garlic Powder
- ½ teaspoon Cumin
- ½ teaspoon Black Pepper
- ⅛ teaspoon of Paprika
- Olive Oil, to coat the pan
- Large Corn or Flour Tortillas
- Mexican Rice and Beans (see Mexican Rice & Beans recipe)
- Taco Sauce, to preference
- Shredded Cheese, to preference

TOTAL TIME 40 MINUTES

SERVES 2

MY PLEASURE COMES FROM GIVING. I LOVE TO COOK FOR OTHERS AND SEE THE SATISFACTION ON THEIR FACES WHEN THEY TAKE A BITE OF MY FOOD.

CHICKEN TERIYAKI STIR FRY

- 2-pounds Chicken Breast
- ½ teaspoon Onion powder
- 1 teaspoon Parsley
- 1 tablespoon All-Purpose Seasoning
- 1 teaspoon Italian Seasoning
- 1 tablespoon Worcestershire Sauce
- ⅛ cup Sriracha Sauce
- 1 tablespoon Spicy Chili Crisp
- 1 teaspoon Minced Garlic
- Vegetable Oil, enough to coat the pan
- 3 Zucchini, sliced
- 3 Bell Peppers, sliced
- 1 Onion, sliced
- 1 stalk Broccoli, chopped
- 1 cup Teriyaki Sauce
- 1 teaspoon Black Pepper

STEP 1. Rinse the chicken with a mix of white vinegar and water, pat dry. Dice the chicken into cubes. Season with onion powder, parsley, all-purpose seasoning, and Italian Seasoning. Rub the seasonings into the chicken. Add Worcestershire sauce, Sriracha, spicy chili crisp and garlic then mix well.

STEP 2. Warm vegetable oil in a wok over medium heat. Toss in the chicken and stir-fry for 10-12 minutes.

STEP 3. Stir-fry the zucchini, peppers, onions, and broccoli. Stir-fry for 3 more minutes. Meanwhile, start the Jasmine Rice (See Jasmine Rice Recipe)

STEP 4. Add the teriyaki sauce to the chicken and veggies, cook over medium heat while stirring. Add more sauce if needed.

STEP 5. Once the chicken has cooked through and the sauce has thickened, serve the stir-fry with a side of Jasmine Rice.

No Waist

BUT TASTE

PESTO CHICKEN

- 1 ½ Chicken Breast
- Olive Oil, enough to coat the pan
- ½ tablespoon Cilantro
- 1 tablespoon Minced Garlic
- ½ teaspoon Black Pepper
- ½ teaspoon Onion Powder
- 6 ounces of Green Beans
- ¼ cup Basil Pesto Sauce
- 10 ounces of Cherry Tomatoes, sliced in half

TOTAL TIME 15 MINUTES

SERVES 4

STEP 1. Rinse the chicken with a mixture of white vinegar and water, then pat dry with a paper towel. Dice the chicken into 1-inch cubes.

STEP 2. Warm olive oil in the sauté pan over medium-high heat, then place the chicken in the pan.
Sprinkle in cilantro, garlic, black pepper, and onion powder. Stir then cook for 5 minutes.

STEP 3. Chop off the ends of the green beans and discard them. Add the green beans to the sauté pan to cook for 6-8 minutes.

STEP 4. Add pesto sauce and cherry tomatoes, then cook for 2-3 minutes more, being careful not to overcook the tomatoes. Remove the pesto chicken from heat, then serve hot.

WHENEVER SOMEONE ASKS WHAT MY PASSION IS, I SAY FASHION IS MY FIRST LOVE, BUT COOKING IS WHERE MY HEART IS.

BUFFALO CAULIFLOWER

- Vegetable Oil, for deep frying
- ¾ cup Flour
- ¼ cup Cornstarch
- ¼ teaspoon Baking Powder
- ⅛ teaspoon Black Pepper
- ½ teaspoon of Garlic Salt
- ⅛ teaspoon Ground White Pepper
- ¾ cups Water
- 1 head of Cauliflower, sliced into florets
- 1 cup Hot Sauce
- 1 stick of Butter

TOTAL TIME 30 MINUTES

SERVES 3-4

STEP 1. Preheat vegetable oil in the frying pan or deep fryer to 350ºF.

STEP 2. In a mixing bowl, add flour, cornstarch, baking powder, black pepper, garlic salt, and ground white pepper, then pour in water. Mix until well combined.

STEP 3. Toss the cauliflower florets in the mixing bowl to coat them. Shake off the excess before frying.

STEP 4. Being careful not to overcrowd the pan, fry the cauliflower florets until golden brown, about 5 minutes.

STEP 5. Heat the hot sauce and butter together in a saucepan. Stir the hot sauce and butter until well combined and the butter has completely melted.

STEP 6. Place the cauliflower florets in a large mixing bowl then pour in the buffalo sauce. Toss the cauliflower in the sauce before serving with veggie sticks and ranch dressing.

CAULIFLOWER FRIED RICE

- 2 Eggs
- ¼ cup Red Onions, diced
- ½ cup Bell Peppers, diced
- 1 ½ cup of Frozen Mixed Vegetables
- 1 tablespoon Parsley
- 2 (20-ounce) bag of Riced Cauliflower (1 head of cauliflower grated)
- 1 ½ tablespoons Soy sauce
- 1 tablespoon Hoisin sauce
- ½ tablespoon Onion Powder
- ½ tablespoon Paprika
- Olive oil, enough to coat the pan

TOTAL TIME 15 MINUTES
SERVES 3-4

STEP 1. Crack two eggs into a small bowl. Beat the eggs well, then set the bowl aside.

STEP 2. In a wok over high heat, sauté the red onions, bell peppers, mixed vegetables and parsley. Cook the vegetables to al dente.

STEP 3. Add the riced cauliflower, soy sauce, hoisin sauce, onion powder, and paprika. Sauté for about 4-5 minutes.

STEP 4. Drizzle olive oil in a separate skillet over medium heat, pour the eggs in and scramble them until about halfway cooked.

STEP 5. Pour the eggs from the skillet into the wok. Scramble the eggs while mixing them into the vegetables. Cook for about 5 more minutes. Serve hot.

CAULIFLOWER LOADED MASH

STEP 1. Preheat the oven to 350ºF. Bring a pot of water to a boil then toss in the cauliflower. Boil the cauliflower until it softens.

STEP 2. Gently whisk butter and heavy whipping cream together in a saucepan over low heat. Once combined, add black pepper, garlic salt, and parsley to the saucepan and simmer until it thickens and the sauce coats the back of a spoon.

STEP 3. Mash the cauliflower in a mixing bowl with a hand masher. DO NOT over mash!

STEP 4. Pour the sauce into the mixing bowl. Gently stir until it has combined with the cauliflower and resembles mashed potatoes.

STEP 5. Use a spoon to scoop the cauliflower mash into a small casserole dish then top it with shredded cheese and chives. Place the mash in the oven to bake for 15 minutes. Serve hot!

- 2 ½ cups Cauliflower Florets (1 head of Cauliflower), chopped
- 1 stick of Butter
- 1 ½ cups Heavy Whipping Cream
- ½ teaspoon Black Pepper
- 1 teaspoon Garlic Salt
- ½ teaspoon Parsley
- Sharp Cheddar Cheese, shredded, to preference
- Chives, to preference

TOTAL TIME 30 MINUTES

SERVES 2

CHICKEN TERIYAKI LETTUCE WRAPS

- Olive Oil, to coat the pan
- 2 Chicken Breasts, diced
- 1 cup Shredded Carrots
- 1 cup Frozen Mixed Vegetables
- 2/3 cup of Chopped White Onion
- ½ teaspoon of Garlic Powder
- ½ teaspoon of Black Pepper
- ½ tablespoon Mrs. Dash
- ½ tablespoon Minced Garlic
- ½ teaspoon of Parsley
- 1 tablespoon Sriracha Sauce
- 1 tablespoon Hoisin Sauce
- 1 teaspoon of Soy Sauce
- Teriyaki Sauce, to preferred taste
- Romaine Lettuce Leaves, for serving

TOTAL TIME 20 MINUTES
SERVES 6

STEP 1. Rinse the chicken with a mixture of white vinegar and water. Dice the chicken breast into small cubes.

STEP 2. Heat olive oil in a wok. Toss in the chicken, then the carrots, mixed vegetables, and white onions. Season with garlic powder, black pepper, Mrs. Dash, minced garlic, and parsley. Lastly, pour in the Sriracha sauce, hoisin sauce, soy sauce, and teriyaki sauce.

STEP 3. Sauté the chicken and vegetables for 8-10 minutes or until the chicken is well done. Turn off the heat.

STEP 4. Serve by spooning a portion of the teriyaki chicken inside of a Romaine leaf. Wrap the lettuce over the teriyaki chicken before eating.

SPICY SALMON BITES

FOR THE SALMON

- 1-pound Salmon, diced
- 1 teaspoon Minced Garlic
- 1 teaspoon Garlic Powder
- 1 teaspoon Parsley
- 1 tablespoon Blackened Seasoning
- 1 teaspoon Cumin

FOR THE SPICY SAUCE

- 2 tablespoons Butter
- 2 tablespoons Sriracha sauce
- 1 ⅓ cup Ketchup
- 1 tablespoon Crushed Red Pepper

TOTAL TIME 10 MINUTES

SERVES 4

FOR THE SALMON

STEP 1. Preheat the oven to 400ºF. After rinsing with a mixture of white vinegar and water, dice the salmon into 1-inch cubes.

STEP 2. Place the salmon in the mixing bowl. Season with minced garlic, garlic powder, parsley, blackened seasoning, and cumin. Add olive oil then mix the seasonings into salmon.

STEP 3. Line a baking sheet with parchment paper. Place the salmon onto the baking sheet. Place the bites equal distance apart. Cover the baking sheet with aluminum foil.

STEP 4. Bake 6-8 minutes covered, then open the oven and take out the baking sheet.
Remove the foil cover and dispose of it. Return the baking sheet to the oven. Bake uncovered for another 6-8 minutes. Take the salmon bites out and turn off the oven.

FOR THE SPICY SAUCE

STEP 5. Whisk butter, Sriracha sauce, ketchup, and crushed red pepper in a small saucepan over high heat until the butter has melted, and the mixture thickens to a sauce. Pour the sauce into a mixing bowl.

STEP 6. Dip and coat the salmon in the spicy sauce. Serve immediately for a quick and delicious appetizer.

SALMON CHEESESTEAK

- 1 ½ pounds Salmon, diced
- Olive Oil, to coat the pan
- ½ Red Bell Pepper, diced
- ½ of a White Onion, chopped
- ½ Orange Bell Pepper, diced
- ½ Green bell pepper
- ½ tablespoon Garlic Salt
- ½ tablespoon Black Pepper
- ½ teaspoon Crushed Red Pepper
- 3 slices of White American Cheese (Shredded Parmesan or Mozzarella option)
- 4 Bolillo Rolls
- Non-stick spray

TOTAL TIME 15-20 MINUTES

SERVES 4

STEP 1. Preheat the oven to 400ºF. Rinse the salmon with a mixture of white vinegar and water. Dice the salmon into cubes.

STEP 2. Heat olive oil in a wok, toss in white onions and bell peppers. Sauté for 2-3 minutes over high heat. Add the salmon then season it with garlic salt, black pepper, and crushed red pepper then cover the pan. Simmer the salmon until the salmon for 5 – 7 minutes.

STEP 3. Take the lid off the pan; add three slices of white American cheese. Continue cooking until the cheese has melted. Stir and sauté the salmon to get it nice and cheesy.

STEP 4. Slice open the bolillo rolls lengthwise. Spread mayonnaise across the inside of the bolillo rolls. Place an equal portion of the salmon cheesesteak inside of each roll, top with parmesan cheese.

STEP 5. Oil a baking sheet with butter or nonstick spray. Place the salmon cheesesteaks on the baking sheet then place them in the oven for 2-3 minutes to toast the bread. Serve and enjoy.

SOUTHWESTERN ZUCCHINI BOATS

- 4 Zucchini
- 2-pounds Ground Turkey
- ½ of a White Onion, diced
- ¼ cup Red Onion, diced
- ¼ cup of Green Bell Peppers, diced
- ½ tablespoon Onion powder
- ½ tablespoon Garlic Powder
- ½ tablespoon Black pepper
- ½ tablespoon Paprika
- ½ tablespoon Parsley
- 1 teaspoon of Minced Garlic
- ½ teaspoon of Garlic Salt
- 2 cups Brown Rice, precooked
- 1 can of Corn (Drained)
- 1 can of Black Beans (Drained)
- 1 can of Diced Tomatoes (Drained)
- Olive Oil, to coat the dish
- ½ cup of Shredded Sharp Cheese
- Mozzarella Cheese, to preference

TOTAL TIME 35 MINUTES

SERVES 8

STEP 1. Preheat the oven to 375ºF. Slice the zucchini in half lengthwise. Use a spoon to scoop the seeds out of each zucchini half to form the shape of a boat.

STEP 2. Place a sauté pan over medium-high heat, then add in the ground turkey, white onions, red onions, and bell peppers. While sautéing, season the ground turkey with onion powder, garlic powder, black pepper, paprika, parsley, minced garlic, and garlic salt. Brown the turkey until it is cooked through with no pink.

STEP 3. Add brown rice, corn, black beans, and tomatoes to the pan. Sauté for an additional 5 minutes.

STEP 4. Coat a baking dish, (preferably glass) with olive oil then line it with parchment paper. Place the zucchini boats onto the parchment paper.

STEP 5. Fill the inside of each zucchini boats with a small amount of ground turkey mixture. Top each boat with shredded cheese. Bake for 15-20 minutes. Remove the zucchini boats from the oven, then serve while hot.

SWEET POTATO FRIES

- 2 Large Sweet Potatoes
- 2 tablespoons of Olive Oil
- 1 tablespoon Cornstarch
- Non Stick Spray
- Cracked Black Pepper, to taste
- Sea Salt, to taste

TOTAL TIME 40 MINUTES

SERVES 4

STEP 1. Preheat the oven to 425ºF. With a peeler or knife, remove the skin from the sweet potatoes. Rinse with water and drain. Slice the sweet potatoes lengthwise into the shape of fries.

STEP 2. Place the sweet potatoes into a mixing bowl then rub a coat of olive oil all over them. Sprinkle in cornstarch then lightly toss the fries.

STEP 3. Oil a baking sheet with olive oil or nonstick spray. Evenly space each fry on the baking pan before placing it into the oven.

STEP 4. Bake for 15 minutes, then remove the fries and turn them over. Return the baking sheet to the oven for another 15 minutes. If you want the fries crispier, allow them to bake for another 3-5 minutes.

STEP 5. Remove the fries from the oven and season them with black pepper and sea salt.

FOIL PACKETS

- 2-pounds Shrimp
- 3-4 Red Potatoes, cube cut
- 4 Foil Packets (Use Aluminum Foil to make the foil packets)
- 4 Andouille Sausages, chopped
- ½ lb. Chicken Breast, diced
- 4 Mini-Ear Corn-on-the-cob
- Mrs. Dash, to taste
- Black Pepper, to taste
- 4 tablespoons Minced Garlic
- 1 tablespoon Butter
- Parsley, to taste

TOTAL TIME 35 MINUTES
SERVES 4

STEP 1. Preheat the oven to 375ºF. Peel and devein the shrimp then rinse with a mixture of white vinegar and water. Cut the potatoes into thick cubes, rinse and drain.

STEP 2. Cut out a rectangular sheet of aluminum foil roughly several inches long. Place an even amount of shrimp, potatoes, sausages, chicken, and one mini ear corn in the center of each foil sheet. Season each foil sheet with Mrs. Dash, black pepper, and minced garlic. Place a tablespoon of butter in each sheet of foil.

STEP 3. Clamp both sides of the foil together in the center. Seal by folding the top edges of the foil down, towards the salmon. Clamp together and fold the side edges of each packet as well. Make sure each packet is fully secure.

STEP 4. Place the packets into the oven to bake for 30 minutes. You will need to use an oven mitten to remove the packets from the oven, they will be steaming hot. DO NOT expose the skin to the steam. Allow the packets to cool briefly. Open the top of each packet before serving.

HONEY SHRIMP WITH BROCCOLI

- 1-pound Shrimp
- 1 teaspoon All-Purpose Seasoning
- 2 teaspoons Minced Garlic
- 2 teaspoons Parsley, chopped
- 2 tablespoons Olive oil
- 1 stalk Broccoli, chopped (or a frozen bag)
- ¼ cup Soy Sauce
- 3 tablespoons Honey
- 1 teaspoon Butter
- ½ tablespoon Sriracha Sauce

TOTAL TIME 35 MINUTES
SERVES 4

STEP 1. Peel and devein shrimp, then rinse with a mixture of white vinegar and water.

STEP 2. In a mixing bowl, coat the shrimp with all-purpose seasoning, 1 teaspoon of minced garlic, and 1 teaspoon of parsley.

STEP 3. Add olive oil to a saucepan, sauté 1 teaspoon each of garlic and parsley until fragrant. Add the shrimp then cook for 2-3 minutes. Add the broccoli, soy sauce, honey, butter, and Sriracha sauce. Sautee for 5-8 minutes on medium low heat until the shrimp is cooked through. Serve immediately.

NOTE: Best served with Jasmine Rice.

I LOVE COOKING FOR THE SAME REASON THAT I LOVE FASHION — THE THRILL OF CREATING SOMETHING NEW.

SALMON SALAD

- 1 Egg
- 2 (6-8 ounce) Salmon fillets
- ½ tablespoon Blackened Seasoning
- ½ teaspoon of Onion powder
- ½ teaspoon of Garlic powder
- 1 teaspoon of Garlic Salt
- Olive Oil, to coat the pan
- 4 handfuls (2-3 cups) Mixed Greens
- ½ cup Dried Cranberries
- ½ cup Cherry Tomatoes, sliced
- ½ cup Sliced Almonds

TOTAL TIME 20 MINUTES

SERVES 2

STEP 1. Bring a small pot of water to a boil before placing the egg inside. Turn off the heat then allow the egg to remain in the hot water for at least 10 minutes. Remove the egg to cool.

STEP 2. Meanwhile, rinse the salmon with a mixture of white vinegar and water, pat dry with a paper towel. Season the fillets with blackened seasoning, onion powder, garlic powder, and garlic salt.

STEP 3. Heat olive oil in a sauté pan over medium-high heat. Sear the filet for 4-5 minutes on each side.

STEP 4. Peel and chop the boiled egg. Toss the egg into the mixing bowl along with mixed greens, dried cranberries, cherry tomatoes, and sliced almonds.

STEP 5. Use a pair of tongs to place a serving of salad on a plate. Slice the salmon into bite-sized pieces or place the whole fillet on top of the salad and use the fork to break it apart as you eat. Serve the salad with your choice of dressing.

STUFFED PEPPERS

- 8 Tricolored Bell Peppers
- 2-pounds of Ground Turkey
- ½ tablespoon Onion powder
- ½ tablespoon Garlic Powder
- ½ tablespoon Black pepper
- ½ tablespoon Paprika
- 1 teaspoon Minced Garlic
- ½ teaspoon Garlic Salt
- 1 ½ cup of Brown Rice pre-cooked
- 1 (15-ounce) can Corn (drained)
- 1 (15-ounce) can Black Beans (drained)
- 1 (14.5-ounce) can diced Tomatoes (drained)
- ½ cupped Red Onion, chopped
- ½ cup of Shredded Cheese
- ½ tablespoon Parsley

TOTAL TIME 50 MINUTES
SERVES 8

STEP 1. Preheat the oven to 375ºF. Chop off only the top of each bell pepper.

STEP 2. Begin sautéing the ground turkey in a pan over medium heat. Season with onion powder, garlic powder, black pepper, paprika, minced garlic, and garlic salt. Cooked for approximately 10 minutes.

STEP 3. Add the brown rice, corn, black beans, tomatoes, and red onion into the sauté pan, cook for 5 minutes.

STEP 4. Stuff each pepper with an equal amount of the ground turkey mixture.

STEP 5. Place the stuffed peppers onto a baking sheet. Sprinkle shredded cheese over top, then place them into the oven. Bake for 35 minutes or until the peppers are tender. Serve with salsa or sour cream and garnished with parsley.

QUICHE CUPS

- 6 Eggs
- 1 tablespoon Milk
- Pinch of Salt
- Pinch of Black Pepper
- Nonstick Spray
- Pinch of Baby Spinach in each cup
- 6 teaspoons Chopped Onions
- 6 teaspoons Sundried Tomatoes
- Shredded Cheese, to taste

TOTAL TIME 10 MINUTES

SERVES 6

STEP 1. Preheat the oven to 375ºF. Crack the eggs into the mixing bowl then pour in the milk. Sprinkle a pinch of salt and pepper into the bowl then beat the eggs.

STEP 2. Use butter or nonstick spray to oil a 6-cup muffin pan. Place a pinch of spinach, onions, sundried tomatoes, and cheese in each cup.

STEP 3. Pour an equal amount of the beaten eggs into each cup then place the muffin pan into the oven to bake for 5-10 minutes. Once a toothpick inserted through the center comes out clean, the quiche cups are ready.

THE KITCHEN IS A PLACE TO EXPERIENCE HAPPY VIBES, MAKE GREAT MEMORIES AND BOND WITH LOVED ONES.

ZUCCHINI FRIES

- 4 Zucchinis, cut into quarters lengthwise
- Nonstick Spray
- 1 cup Panko Breadcrumbs
- ½ cup Parmesan Cheese, grated
- 1 teaspoon Italian Seasoning
- Kosher Salt, to taste
- Black Pepper, to taste
- ½ cup Flour
- 2 Eggs, beaten
- 2 tablespoons Parsley Leaves, chopped

TOTAL TIME 30 MINUTES

SERVES 6

STEP 1. Preheat the oven to 425ºF. Rinse the zucchini and slice them into the shape of fries.

STEP 2. Coat a wire rack with nonstick spray and place it on a baking sheet then set it aside.

STEP 3. In a large bowl, combine Panko breadcrumbs, Parmesan, and Italian seasoning; season with salt and pepper, to taste. Set the mixing bowl aside.

STEP 4. Beat 2 eggs in a separate bowl.

STEP 5. Working in batches, dip the zucchini in flour, next dip it into the eggs, then dip it in the Panko mixture, pressing to coat.

STEP 6. Place the zucchini onto the prepared baking sheet. Place into the oven and bake for 20 minutes, or until golden brown and crisp. Serve immediately, garnished with parsley, if desired.

You're
JUST A SIDE

CHEESY GARLIC BREAD

- ½ tablespoon Olive Oil
- ½ tablespoon Cilantro
- ½ tablespoon Parsley
- ½ tablespoon Garlic Paste
- 5 tablespoons Unsalted Butter, softened
- 1 loaf of Bread
- ½ cup Italian Shredded Cheese Blend
- ½ cup Parmesan Cheese shredded
- ⅛ cup Parmesan Cheese grated

TOTAL TIME 10 MINUTES

SERVES 6-8

STEP 1. Preheat the oven to 400ºF. In a mixing bowl, use a wooden spoon to press the olive oil, cilantro, parsley, and garlic paste into the unsalted butter, creating the spread.

STEP 2. Slice the loaf in half, then use a spatula to generously spread the paste inside of the bread.

STEP 3. Sprinkle all of the cheeses over the paste.

STEP 4. Bake the cheesy garlic bread on an oiled sheet pan for 5-8 minutes, or until lightly toasted and golden brown. Cool slightly before cutting and serving.

NOTE: Add cheese to your liking. I like mine extra cheesy!

YELLOW RICE

STEP 1. Preheat a sauté pan over medium heat. Sauté the minced garlic for 1 minute. Add crushed bay leaves, Mrs. Dash, cumin, Italian seasoning, turmeric and garlic salt, stir continuously.

STEP 2. Pour the chicken stock into to the pan while stirring. Add the rice, then the butter and chicken bouillon cube. Stir the ingredients for 1-2 minutes.

STEP 3. Cover the pan and simmer the rice for 20-25 minutes. Stir occasionally. Cook the rice to al dente. Serve hot. Makes a great side for oxtails or curry.

- 1 tablespoon Minced Garlic
- 2 Bay Leaves, crushed
- 1 teaspoon Mrs. Dash
- 1 teaspoon Cumin
- 1 teaspoon Italian Seasoning
- 2 teaspoons Turmeric Powder
- ⅛ teaspoon Garlic Salt
- 3 cups Chicken Stock
- 4 Cups Jasmine Rice
- 3 tablespoons Butter
- 1 Chicken Bouillon Cube

TOTAL TIME 30 MINUTES

SERVES 4-6

HOME-COOKED MEALS CAN BE EASY, FUN, AND VERY REWARDING.

GARLIC MASHED POTATOES

- 6-8 Red Potatoes, chopped
- Pinch of Salt
- 1 tablespoon Butter
- ½ tablespoon Garlic Powder
- 1 ½ teaspoon Garlic Salt
- 1 ½ teaspoon Black Pepper
- 1 tablespoon Parsley
- ½ cup Half and Half Milk
- 2 cups Heavy Whipping Cream
- 2 tablespoons Garlic Paste
- 2 tablespoons Squeezed Butter

TOTAL TIME 30-35 MINUTES

SERVES 6-8

STEP 1. Boil the potatoes in a pot of water with a pinch of salt until they have softened then drain them in a strainer. Return the potatoes to the pot. Add a tablespoon of butter then mash the potatoes with a potato masher or fork.

STEP 2. Season the mashed potatoes with garlic powder, garlic salt, black pepper, and parsley. Pour in half and half milk and heavy whipping cream, then stir in the garlic paste and squeezed butter.

STEP 3. Use a mixer to whip the potatoes for 2 minutes or until the mashed potatoes are smooth, fluffy, and without chunks. Keep the potatoes covered until serving.

ROASTED RUSSET POTATOES

- 3-4 Russet Potatoes
- 1 tablespoon Olive Oil
- 1 teaspoon Garlic Salt
- 2 teaspoon Mrs. Dash
- 1 teaspoon Italian Seasoning

TOTAL TIME 35 MINUTES

SERVES 4-6

STEP 1. Preheat the oven to 400ºF. Rinse then cut the potatoes into quarters. Place the potatoes into a baking pan then rub olive oil, evenly, over all of the potatoes. Season them with garlic salt, Mrs. Dash, and Italian seasoning.

STEP 2. Cover the baking pan with foil, then bake the potatoes for 30-35 minutes or until the potatoes have softened.

STEP 3. Cool the potatoes for 10 minutes then serve.

COLLARD GREENS

- 4 bunches Collard Greens
- 2 bunches Mustard Greens
- 4 tablespoons Olive Oil
- 1 tablespoon Minced Garlic
- ¾ cup Tri-colored Bell Peppers, diced
- ¼ cup White Onions, diced
- 1-2 precooked Smoked Turkey legs
- 5 cups Chicken Stock
- 2 ½ cups Water
- 1 tablespoon Garlic Salt
- ½ tablespoon Black Pepper
- ½ tablespoon Paprika
- 1 tablespoon Old Bay seasoning
- ½ tablespoon Onion Powder
- 1 teaspoon Crushed Red Pepper
- 4 tablespoons Butter

TOTAL TIME 1.5 HOURS
SERVES 10-12

STEP 1. Remove the stems from the collard and mustard greens. Rinse the leaves of the greens with cool water then chop them into bite-sized pieces. Place the greens into a large mixing bowl.

STEP 2. Warm the olive oil over high heat in the stockpot. Add the minced garlic, bell peppers, onions, and smoked turkey to the stockpot. Sauté the ingredients for 6 minutes.

STEP 3. Deglaze the pot by pouring in one cup of the chicken stock. Fit the greens into the pot, then pour in the water and the rest of the chicken stock. Simmer the greens for 30 minutes.

STEP 4. Season the greens with garlic salt, black pepper, paprika, Old Bay seasoning, onion powder, crushed red pepper, and butter. Use a pair of tongs to toss the greens in the pot. Simmer over medium heat for 45-50 minutes. Serve hot. They taste great with meatloaf and mashed potatoes!

CREAMY CORN

- 2 tablespoons Butter
- 2 (15.25-ounce) cans Sweet Corn (drained)
- ⅛ cup Cornstarch
- 1 tablespoon Cream Cheese (Optional)
- 1 cup Heavy Whipping Cream
- ½ teaspoon Black Pepper
- ¼ teaspoon Garlic Salt
- ¼ teaspoon Onion Powder
- 1 tablespoon Cilantro or Parsley
- ¼ teaspoon Garlic Powder

TOTAL TIME 15-20 MINUTES

SERVES 3-6

STEP 1. Warm the butter in a saucepan over medium heat. Drain the liquid from the cans of corn, then add the corn to the saucepan. Stir in the cornstarch and combine well.

STEP 2. Toss in the cream cheese, then pour in the heavy whipping cream while stirring. Season with black pepper, garlic salt, onion powder, parsley, and garlic powder.

STEP 3. Cook the creamy corn for 10 minutes while stirring occasionally. Serve this as a side dish with fried chicken!

NOTE: You must add the cornstarch first and ensure that its mixed completely into the corn. This will prevent the creamy corn from becoming too watery. The heavy cream and cream cheese will make it extra creamy!

GREEN BEANS

- 1lb of Fresh Green Beans
- 2 tablespoons of Olive Oil
- ⅛ teaspoon of Garlic Salt
- ¼ teaspoon of Black Pepper
- ¼ teaspoon of Garlic Powder

TOTAL TIME 10 MINUTES
SERVES 4

STEP 1. Rinse the green beans then cut and discard their ends.

STEP 2. Warm olive oil in a sauté pan over medium heat then toss in the green beans.

STEP 3. Season the green beans with garlic salt, black pepper, and garlic powder. Sauté for 10 minutes or until al dente.

STEP 4. Serve this quick and healthy side garnished with sea salt and cracked pepper.

I DEVELOPED A LOVE AND PASSION FOR COOKING IN MY GRANDMOTHER'S KITCHEN.

ASPARAGUS

STEP 1. Rinse the asparagus and pat dry. Cut and discard the rough, woody ends.

STEP 2. Warm olive oil in a sauté pan over medium heat then toss in the asparagus.

STEP 3. Season the asparagus with minced garlic, garlic salt, and black pepper.

STEP 4. Sauté the asparagus over medium heat for 5 -7 minutes or until al dente. Serve and enjoy!

- 1 large bunch of Asparagus
- 2 tablespoons Olive Oil
- 1 ½ teaspoons Minced Garlic
- ⅛ teaspoon Garlic Salt
- ¼ teaspoon Black Pepper

TOTAL TIME 10 MINUTES

SERVES 4

SWEET POTATO CASSEROLE

FOR THE CRUMB TOPPING

- ⅓ cup Brown Sugar
- ¼ teaspoon Ground Cinnamon
- ⅛ cup of Flour
- ½ cup Pecans, chopped
- ¼ cup Melted Butter
- ⅛ teaspoon Nutmeg

FOR THE SWEET POTATOES

- 4-5 Sweet Potatoes, sliced (half-moon cut)
- Pinch of Salt
- ⅓ cup Brown Sugar
- ⅓ cup White Sugar
- 1 teaspoon Cinnamon
- 1 teaspoon Vanilla Extract
- ¼ teaspoon Nutmeg
- ⅓ cup Melted Butter
- Nonstick Spray

TOTAL TIME 45 MINUTES

SERVES 4-6

FOR THE CRUMB TOPPING

STEP 1. In a mixing bowl, add the brown sugar, cinnamon, flour, pecans, melted butter, and nutmeg. Use clean hands to mix and crumble the ingredients together.

FOR THE SWEET POTATOES

STEP 2. Preheat the oven to 400ºF. Peel and chop the sweet potatoes, then rinse and drain them in a strainer. Boil the sweet potatoes and salt in a medium-sized pot for 15-20 minutes or until they have softened. Drain the water then place the potatoes into a mixing bowl and lightly mash with a potato masher or fork.

STEP 3. Use a hand mixer to whip the potatoes for 1- 2 minutes, bringing them to a smooth purée without any stringiness.

STEP 4. Use a large spoon to mix the brown sugar, white sugar, cinnamon, vanilla, nutmeg, and melted butter into the purée.

STEP 5. Generously grease a small casserole dish with non-stick spray then pour in the sweet potato purée. Spread the crumb topping evenly over the top.

STEP 6. Place the casserole dish into the oven to bake for 30-35 minutes. Allow to the casserole to cool for 15 minutes before serving. Enjoy!

MAC & CHEESE

STEP 1. Preheat the oven to 350ºF. In a large pot, boil the macaroni to al dente.

STEP 2. Drain the macaroni using a strainer then pour the macaroni into a casserole dish. Season the macaroni with Old Bay seasoning, black pepper, and garlic salt. Stir the ingredients until they are well combined.

STEP 3. Crack the egg into a bowl then whisk it. Stir the beaten egg and the milk into the macaroni.

STEP 4. Add the cream of mushroom, butter, and heavy cream then sprinkle in all of the cheeses. Using a large spoon, stir the ingredients until well combined. Sprinkle more on the top.

STEP 5. Cover with foil then place the mac and cheese into the oven to bake. After 20-25 minutes, remove the foil and allow the top of the Mac & Cheese to brown for 5 more minutes. Cool for 10 minutes before serving.

- 1-1 ½ lbs Macaroni Elbows
- ¼ teaspoon Old Bay Seasoning
- ¼ teaspoon Black Pepper
- ¼ teaspoon Garlic Salt
- 1 Egg
- 2 cups Milk
- 1 can Cream of Mushroom, Chicken, or Celery, optional
- ½ stick Butter
- ¼ cup Heavy Whipping Cream
- 2 cups Extra Sharp Cheddar, grated
- 2 cups Regular Sharp Cheddar, grated
- 2 cups Medium Cheddar, grated
- 2 cups Colby Jack, grated
- 2 cups Monterrey Jack, grated

TOTAL TIME 45 MINUTES

SERVES 6

AU GRATIN POTATOES

- Nonstick Spray

FOR THE POTATOES

- 3-4 Russet Potatoes
- ¼ teaspoon Paprika
- ¼ teaspoon Parsley

FOR THE CHEESE SAUCE

- 1 tablespoons Butter (1 additional tablespoon, optional)
- 1 cup White Onions chopped
- ¼ cup of Flour
- 1 ½ cups Heavy Whipping Cream
- 1 teaspoon Black Pepper
- 1 teaspoon Onion Powder
- ¼ teaspoon Cayenne pepper
- ¼ teaspoon Garlic Salt
- 1 ½ cup Sharp Cheddar Cheese, shredded

TOTAL TIME 40 MINUTES

SERVES 4-6

FOR THE POTATOES

STEP 1. Rinse and peel the potatoes. Thinly slice the potatoes then set them aside in a bowl of water for the time being. This is done to keep them from turning brown.

FOR THE CHEESE SAUCE

STEP 2. Warm the butter in a sauté pan over medium heat. Add the white onions and sauté them for 1-2 minutes or until caramelized. Stir the flour into the onions until fully incorporated. Continue to stir and cook for 1 more minute.

STEP 3. Pour in the heavy whipping cream then whisk the mixture for roughly 30 seconds. Add the black pepper, onion powder, cayenne pepper, and garlic salt, then whisk continuously on low heat for 2-3 minutes. Sprinkle in the sharp cheddar then whisk continuously for another 2-3 minutes.

STEP 4. Spray a casserole dish with nonstick cooking spray. Place a thin layer of potatoes to the bottom of the dish. Pour the cheese sauce over the potatoes then repeat the process. Sprinkle a thin layer of shredded cheese followed by, paprika, and then parsley over the top layer.

STEP 5. Cover the baking pan with foil, then bake at 400ºF for 30-40 minutes or until the potatoes have cooked thoroughly. Remove from the oven and rest for at least 15 minutes before serving.

NOTE: Shredded cheese can be added to each layer's cheese sauce for extra cheesy au gratin potatoes!

ROASTED ROSEMARY POTATOES

STEP 1. Preheat the oven to 400ºF. Rinse and cut the potatoes into quarters before placing them in a medium sized baking dish. Coat the potatoes with olive oil to help prevent them from sticking to the dish.

STEP 2. Toss the potatoes in the garlic salt, Mrs. Dash, and Italian seasoning then place the butter into the dish. Remove the stems from the rosemary and evenly sprinkle the leaves around in the baking dish.

STEP 3. Cover the baking dish with aluminum foil and seal the corners. Bake for 35 minutes or until the potatoes have softened.

STEP 4. Use a knife to check the texture of the potatoes. They are done when a knife easily slices through the center. Remove the potatoes from the oven and serve once slightly cooled.

- 4-6 Red Potatoes, cut into quarters
- Olive Oil (for coating the potatoes)
- ¼ teaspoon Garlic Salt
- 1 teaspoon Mrs. Dash
- 1 teaspoon Italian Seasoning
- 1 teaspoon Butter
- 2 sprigs Rosemary

TOTAL TIME 40-45 MINUTES

SERVES 4-6

HONEY BUTTERED CORNBREAD

- 1 cup Flour, leveled
- ¾ cup Cornmeal
- ½ teaspoon Kosher Salt
- ½ teaspoon Baking Soda
- 1 teaspoon Baking Powder
- 1 stick of Butter
- ¼ cup Vegetable oil
- 1 cup Sugar
- ⅓ cup Honey
- 2 Eggs
- 1 ¼ cups Buttermilk

TOTAL TIME 40 MINUTES

SERVES 6

STEP 1. Preheat the oven to 375ºF. In a small mixing bowl, combine the flour, cornmeal, kosher salt, baking soda, and baking powder.

STEP 2. Melt the butter in a large bowl in the microwave. Add the vegetable oil, sugar, and honey to the bowl with the melted butter. Stir until well combined.

STEP 3. Crack the eggs into the bowl, then pour in the buttermilk. Whisk thoroughly.

STEP 4. Stir the dry ingredients (cornmeal, kosher salt, baking soda, and baking powder) into the wet ingredients but DO NOT over mix! Make sure all of the ingredients are completely combined but don't worry if there are a few lumps.

STEP 5. Use nonstick spray to grease the bottom and sides of a baking pan that is approximately 8x8 inches.

STEP 6. Pour the batter into the baking pan and smooth out the top. Bake for 30 minutes. The cornbread is done when a toothpick inserted through its center comes out clean with no batter on it. Allow the cornbread to cool for 10 minutes before slicing and serving.

CANDIED YAMS

STEP 1. Preheat the oven to 350ºF. Peel the sweet potatoes. Rinse then cut the sweet potatoes into approximately 1 inch slices.

STEP 2. Boil the sweet potatoes in a pot until they have softened. Drain the water with a strainer then place the sweet potatoes in a baking dish.

STEP 3. Combine the butter, cinnamon, brown sugar, white sugar, and nutmeg in a saucepan and warm the mixture over high heat until it thickens into a syrup.

STEP 4. Fully coat the sweet potatoes with syrup. Cover the baking dish with foil. Place it in the oven to bake for 30 minutes or until tender and golden brown on top.

STEP 5. Remove the yams for the oven and cool before serving.

- 4 Sweet Potatoes
- ½ stick of Butter
- 1 teaspoon Cinnamon
- ¾ cup Brown Sugar
- ½ cup White Sugar
- ¼ teaspoon Nutmeg

TOTAL TIME 45 MINUTES

SERVING SIZE 6

BLACK-EYED PEAS

- 1-pound bag Black-Eyed Peas, dried
- 5 cups Chicken Stock
- 2 ½ cups Water
- 4 tablespoons Butter
- ¼ cup White Onions
- ¼ cup Tricolored Bell Peppers
- 1 tablespoon Minced Garlic
- 1 Smoked Turkey Leg
- 1 tablespoon Garlic Salt
- ½ tablespoon Paprika
- ½ tablespoon Black Pepper
- 1 tablespoon Old Bay seasoning
- ½ tablespoon Onion Powder

TOTAL TIME 1.5 HOURS

SERVES 6

STEP 1. Soak the black-eyed peas in at least three cups of water for 3-4 hours before cooking. (If you do not soak the peas, they will take much longer to cook.) Discard the water and rinse the peas.

STEP 2. Pour the black-eyed peas, chicken stock, and water into the stockpot. Warm the stockpot over medium-high heat.

STEP 3. Add the butter, onions, bell peppers, minced garlic, and smoked turkey. Stir the ingredients until well combined.

STEP 4. Season the black-eyed peas with garlic salt, paprika, black pepper, Old Bay seasoning, and onion powder. Use a large spoon to thoroughly mix the ingredients in the pot.

STEP 5. Cover the stockpot. Simmer on low-medium heat for one hour so the peas can soak in all of the flavor.

STEP 6. Once the peas are tender, remove the stockpot from the heat. Use a ladle to scoop the black-eyed peas into a bowl when serving.

SOUR CREAM & CHEDDAR MASH

- 6-7 Russet Potatoes
- 2 cloves Garlic
- 1 Chicken Bouillon Cube
- 1 teaspoon Garlic Paste
- 2 tablespoons Butter
- 1 ¼ cup Heavy Whipping Cream
- 1 cup of Sour Cream
- ½ teaspoon Garlic Salt
- ½ teaspoon Black Pepper
- 1 ½ cup Cheddar Cheese shredded
- 1 tablespoon Chives

TOTAL TIME 40 MINUTES
SERVES 6

STEP 1. Preheat the oven to 350ºF. Peel and rinse the potatoes.

STEP 2. Bring a pot of water to a boil. Drop the garlic cloves, bouillon cube and potatoes into the pot. Cook until completely softened. Use a strainer to drain the water.

STEP 3. Return the potatoes to the pot. Use a potato masher to mash the potatoes. Add garlic paste, butter, heavy whipping cream, and sour cream into the pot. Use a hand mixer to whip the potatoes.

STEP 4. Season the mashed potatoes with garlic salt, and black pepper. Whip the mashed potatoes until they are creamy and without lumps.

STEP 5. Spread a layer of the potatoes into the casserole dish. Top the layer with cheddar cheese and chives then repeat.

STEP 6. Place the casserole dish into the oven to bake for 10-12 minutes. The cheese should be melted and slightly bubbly. Serve immediately.

ELOTE MEXICAN CORN

- pinch Garlic Salt
- Fresh Corn on the Cob (to preference)
- Mexican Crema (add to preference)
- Mayonnaise (add to preference)
- Cotija Cheese grated (add to preference) (can use parmesan as substitute)
- Queso Fresco Crumbles, optional (use a generous amount on each corn skewer)
- Skewers (1 for each corn on the cob)
- Squeezed Butter (add to preference)
- Cayenne Pepper, to taste (can substitute with paprika for less spice)
- Parsley, chopped (add to preference)

TOTAL TIME 15 MINUTES

STEP 1. Bring water to a boil in a stockpot. Sprinkle in a pinch of garlic salt before adding the corn to the water.

STEP 2. Boil the corn for 5-8 minutes.

STEP 3. Use a small bowl to combine the crema and mayonnaise. Spread the grated cotija cheese and Queso Fresco crumbles on a plate.

STEP 4. Insert one skewer into each corn on the cob. Use a brush to evenly spread the squeezed butter and then the mixture of crema and mayo all over each cob. Roll the corn in the cotija and queso to evenly coat the whole ear.

STEP 5. Finish by sprinkling each cob with cayenne pepper, a little more queso fresco, and parsley.

MEXICAN RICE & BEANS

FOR THE RICE

STEP 1. Warm the olive oil in the sauté pan over medium-high heat. Sauté the cilantro, onion, and garlic for 1-2 minutes.

STEP 2. Add the jasmine rice. Sauté it for just 2-3 minutes before pouring in 4 1/2 cups of water. Next, include a chicken and tomato bouillon cube and tomato paste. Stir, stir, stir!

STEP 3. Sprinkle in the garlic salt and cayenne pepper and stir once more. Reduce the heat to low. Cover the pan and simmer for 25-30 minutes.

FOR THE BEANS

STEP 4. Warm the olive oil in a large pot over medium heat then cook the onions, garlic, and cilantro for two minutes. Drain the beans. Add the beans, pour in the chicken stock, and toss in the chicken bouillon. Stir well.

STEP 5. Boil the pinto beans over medium-high heat for 15 minutes. To serve, you can combine the beans and rice in one serving bowl or enjoy them separately.

FOR THE RICE

- Olive Oil, to coat the pan
- ⅛ cup Cilantro, chopped
- ½ of an Onion, sliced thin
- ½ teaspoon Fresh Garlic
- 4 Cups Jasmine Rice
- 4 ½ cup of Water
- 1 Chicken Bouillon Cube
- 1 Tomato Bouillon Cube
- 1 (6-ounce) can of Tomato Paste
- ¼ teaspoon Garlic Salt
- ¼ teaspoon Cayenne Pepper

FOR THE BEANS

- 2 tablespoons Olive Oil
- ½ cup White Onions, minced
- ½ teaspoon Fresh Garlic
- 2 tbsp Cilantro, chopped
- 2 cans of Pinto Beans
- 2 cups Chicken Stock
- 1 Chicken Bouillon Cube

TOTAL TIME 45 MINUTES

SERVES 6

Simply
SNACKIN'

SALMON TACOS

- 4-6 Corn or Flour tortillas
- Olive Oil (just enough to coat the pan)

FOR THE TACO SAUCE

- ½ cup Ranch Dressing
- ¼ cup Sriracha Sauce (increase the Sriracha for more spice)

FOR THE SALMON

- 1 ½-pound Fillet of Salmon
- ½ tablespoon Old Bay Seasoning
- 1 tablespoon Blackened Seasoning
- ½ tablespoon Onion Powder
- ½ teaspoon Garlic Powder
- Olive Oil, to coat the pan

FOR THE COLESLAW

- 3 cups Coleslaw mix
- 1 Lime
- ⅛ cup Cilantro, chopped
- ⅛ cup Jalapeno, chopped
- ⅛ cup Red Onions, diced
- 1 teaspoon Black Pepper
- 1 tablespoon Honey

TOTAL TIME 10 MINUTES

SERVES 4-6

FOR THE TACO SAUCE

STEP 1. In a small mixing bowl, combine the ranch dressing and Sriracha sauce to make the taco sauce.

FOR THE SALMON

STEP 2. Rinse the salmon with a mix of white vinegar and water, pat dry with a paper towel. Dice the salmon into 1-inch cubes.

STEP 3. Place the salmon in a mixing bowl. Season with Old Bay seasoning, blackened seasoning, onion powder, and garlic powder.

STEP 4. Warm a sauté pan over medium-high heat. Drizzle in olive oil then place the salmon into the pan, cook for 4-6 minutes.

FOR THE COLESLAW

STEP 5. Add coleslaw mix to a large mixing bowl, then squeeze the juice of one whole lime into the bowl. Add cilantro, jalapeno, red onion, black pepper, and honey then mix well.

STEP 6. Warm a griddle pan over medium heat. Cook the tortillas on one side for 1-2 minutes, flip, then repeat.

STEP 7. Place a portion of salmon in each tortilla then drizzle the homemade taco sauce over the salmon. Serve immediately while the salmon is still warm.

SHRIMP TACOS

STEP 1. Peel and devein the shrimp then clean them by rinsing with a mixture of white vinegar and water.

STEP 2. Place the shrimp in a mixing bowl then add the seasonings (old bay, cilantro, paprika, cumin, cayenne, and garlic). Toss the shrimp in the bowl to fully coat with seasoning.

STEP 3. Warm olive oil in a sauté pan over medium heat, place the seasoned shrimp in the pan and sear them for 5-8 minutes. Stir occasionally.

STEP 4. Warm a griddle pan over medium heat, then cook the tortillas for 1-2 minutes on each side. Serve with a portion of shrimp inside each tortilla, topped with mango salsa. (see next recipe).

NOTE: It's best to have a taco divider to separate the tortillas when placing the shrimp and salsa inside the tortilla.

FOR THE SHRIMP

- 2-pounds Shrimp
- 1 tablespoon Old Bay Seasoning
- ⅛ cup Cilantro, chopped
- ½ tablespoon Paprika
- ½ tablespoon Cumin
- ¼ teaspoon Cayenne Pepper
- 1 tablespoon Garlic, chopped
- Olive Oil, to coat the pan

FOR THE TACOS

- 4-6 Corn or Flour Tortillas

TOTAL TIME 15 MINUTES

SERVES 4-6

MANGO SALSA

- 1 lime
- 1 large Mango (2 small mangos), diced
- 1 Green Bell Pepper, diced
- 1 Red Bell Pepper, diced
- 1 Red Onion, diced
- 1 Jalapeno, diced (optional)

TOTAL TIME 15 MINUTES

SERVES 4-6

STEP 1. Peel and dice the mango. Dice the bell peppers, red onion, and jalapeno. Remove the jalapeno's seeds to reduce the spice.

STEP 2. Toss the ingredients together in a mixing bowl until well combined. Squeeze lime over the contents. Sprinkle in a pinch of salt and pepper to finish. Serve chilled with tortilla chips.

MY PLEASURE COMES FROM GIVING. I LOVE TO COOK FOR OTHERS AND SEE THE SATISFACTION ON THEIR FACES WHEN THEY TAKE A BITE OF MY FOOD.

JERK CHICKEN TACOS

FOR THE TACO SAUCE

STEP 1. In a small mixing bowl, combine the ranch dressing and Sriracha sauce to make the taco sauce.

FOR THE CHICKEN

STEP 2. Rinse the chicken breast with a mixture of white vinegar and water. Remove the chicken's fat then dice the chicken into 1-inch cubes.

STEP 3. Place the chicken into a mixing bowl then season with jerk seasoning, black pepper, and onion powder. Add garlic, bell peppers, onions, and cilantro. Mix the chicken breast together with the other ingredients.

STEP 4. Warm the olive oil in a sauté pan over medium heat. Cook the chicken breast mixture for 7-10 minutes or until the chicken has cooked through.

FOR THE COLESLAW

STEP 5. Add coleslaw mix to a large mixing bowl, then squeeze the juice of one whole lime into the bowl. Add cilantro, jalapeno, red onion, black pepper, and honey then mix well.

STEP 6. Heat olive oil in a griddle pan, then cook the tortillas 1-2 minutes on each side. Place a portion of chicken in each tortilla, then drizzle the homemade taco sauce over the chicken. Serve promptly while the chicken is still warm.

- Olive Oil (just enough to coat the pan)
- Corn or Flour Tortillas

FOR THE TACO SAUCE

- ½ cup Ranch Dressing
- ¼ cup Sriracha Sauce (increase the amount of Sriracha sauce for more spice)

FOR THE CHICKEN

- 2 Chicken Breasts
- 2 tablespoons Jerk Seasoning
- ¼ teaspoon Black Pepper
- ½ tablespoon Onion powder
- 4 cloves Garlic, chopped
- ½ cup Green Bell Peppers, chopped
- ½ cup White Onions, chopped
- ⅛ cup of Cilantro, chopped
- 2 tbsp Olive Oil, divided

FOR THE COLESLAW

- 3 cups Coleslaw mix
- ⅛ cup Cilantro, chopped
- ⅛ cup Jalapeno, chopped
- ⅛ cup Red Onions, diced
- 1 teaspoon Black Pepper
- 1 tablespoon Honey
- 1 Lime

TOTAL TIME 15 MINUTES

SERVES 4-6

CHEESESTEAK EGG ROLLS

- 1 Egg (for Egg Wash)
- 1 tablespoon Olive Oil
- 1 White Onion, chopped
- 1 Green Bell Pepper, chopped
- 2-pounds, Steak Umm Sliced Steak or Shredded Roast Beef
- ½ teaspoon Seasoned Salt
- Pinch of Black Pepper
- ⅛ teaspoon Garlic Salt
- ½ teaspoon Garlic Powder
- ½ teaspoon Onion Powder
- 1 cup Shredded Mozzarella Cheese
- 16 Egg Roll Wraps
- 1 cup Shredded Parmesan Cheese
- Vegetable Oil (enough to fully cover the egg rolls)

TOTAL TIME 30 MINUTES
SERVES 4

STEP 1. Crack the egg into a bowl. Add a tablespoon of water then beat the egg to create the egg wash. Set aside.

STEP 2. Warm the olive in a sauté pan over low heat. Sauté the onions, bell pepper, and steak together. Use a spatula to chop the steak down to bite-sized pieces as you sauté.

STEP 3. Season the mixture with seasoned salt, black pepper, garlic salt, garlic powder, onion powder. Continue to sauté until the steak is no longer pink. Drain the oil from the saucepan then place the steak in a mixing bowl.

STEP 4. Add mozzarella cheese to the steak then toss the mixture together to combine.

STEP 5. Use two wraps for each roll. Place the wraps in a diamond shape onto a flat surface. Brush each wraps' outer edges with egg wash.

STEP 6. Place an equal portion of the steak mixture in the center of each wrap, then sprinkle parmesan cheese over top. Fold the side corners inward, fold the bottom corner over the two folded sides, then roll upwards towards the top corner until the egg roll is formed.

STEP 7. Warm vegetable oil to 350ºF in a large frying pan or deep fryer. Fry the egg rolls until they are crispy and golden brown. Be careful not to overcrowd the pan.

STEP 8. Pull the egg rolls out the fryer, sit them on a wire rack to drain all excess oil. These egg rolls are best served with sweet chili sauce for dipping.

LA-STYLE STREET TACOS

FOR THE TACO SAUCE

STEP 1. In a small mixing bowl, combine the ranch dressing and Sriracha sauce to make the taco sauce.

FOR THE CHICKEN

STEP 2. Rinse the chicken breast with a mixture of white vinegar and water. Pat dry with a paper towel. Dice each chicken breast into 1-inch cubes.

STEP 3. Place the chicken into a mixing bowl and season with onion powder, garlic powder, cumin, black pepper, paprika, and Salsa Verde.

STEP 4. Warm the olive oil in a sauté pan then sauté for 10-12 minutes or until the chicken is cooked through.

STEP 5. Heat olive oil in a griddle pan, then cook the tortillas 1-2 minutes on each side. Place a portion of chicken in each tortilla, followed by coleslaw. Drizzle the homemade taco sauce over the tacos. Serve promptly while the chicken is still warm.

FOR THE TACO SAUCE

- ½ cup Ranch Dressing
- ¼ cup Sriracha Sauce (increase the amount of sriracha sauce for more spice)

FOR THE CHICKEN

- 2 chicken Breasts
- ½ teaspoon Onion Powder
- ½ teaspoon Garlic Powder
- ½ teaspoon Cumin
- ½ teaspoon Black Pepper
- ⅛ teaspoon Paprika
- ½ cup of Salsa Verde
- 1 tbsp Extra Virgin Olive Oil

FOR THE TACOS

- 4-6 Street Taco Tortillas
- Olive Oil (enough to coat the pan)

TOTAL TIME 15 MINUTES

SERVES 4-6

ASIAN ZING WINGS

- 4-6 cups Vegetable Oil (enough to cover the wings)
- ¾ cup Sweet Chili
- ¾ cup Sriracha sauce
- 2-pounds Party Wings

TOTAL TIME 15 MINUTES
SERVES 4

STEP 1. Preheat vegetable oil in the frying pan or deep fryer to 350ºF.

STEP 2. Mix the sweet chili sauce and Sriracha sauce together in a small bowl

STEP 3. Rinse the Party wings with a mixture of white vinegar and water. Pat dry. Fry the bare chicken wings for 8-10 minutes or until they have thoroughly cooked, the wings should be crisp and golden-brown.

STEP 4. Drain any excess oil using the wire rack. Inspect the inside of each chicken wing for any sign of undercooked meat. If it has cooked through, move on to the next step.

STEP 5. Toss the wings in the desired amount of Asian Zing sauce. Once the wings are evenly coated, serve and enjoy!

MANGO HABANERO WINGS

- 4-6 cups Vegetable Oil (enough to cover the wings)
- 2 Mangos, sliced
- 2 Habanero Peppers
- 1 ½ Cup of Water
- Sea Salt, to taste
- Black Pepper, to taste
- 2-pounds of Party wings
- 2 tablespoons of Olive Oil
- Vegetable Oil

TOTAL TIME 15 MINUTES

SERVES 4

STEP 1. Preheat vegetable oil in the frying pan or deep fryer to 350ºF.

STEP 2. Peel the mangos and give them a rough chop. If you have a gas stove, use tongs to roast the habanero peppers over medium fire for approximately 1 minute. Alternatively, preheat the oven to 400ºF and roast the habaneros on a sheet of foil for 2-3 minutes.

STEP 3. Add the mangos, habaneros, and water to the blender and purée to an even and smooth consistency. Pour the purée into a bowl. Add salt and pepper.

STEP 4. Rinse the party wings with a mixture of white vinegar and water. Pat dry. Fry the bare chicken wings for 8-10 minutes or until they have thoroughly cooked, the wings should be crisp and golden-brown.

STEP 5. Drain any excess oil from the chicken using a wire rack. Inspect the inside of each chicken wing for any sign of undercooked meat. If it has cooked through, move on to the next step.

STEP 6. Toss the wings in the desired amount of mango habanero sauce. Once the wings are evenly coated, serve and enjoy!

BUFFALO WINGS

- 4-6 cups Vegetable Oil (enough to cover the wings)
- 1 cup Hot Sauce
- 1 stick of Butter
- 2-pounds Party Wings

TOTAL TIME 10 MINUTES

SERVES 4

STEP 1. Preheat vegetable oil in the frying pan or deep fryer to 350ºF.

STEP 2. Heat the hot sauce and butter in a saucepan over medium-low heat. Stir and warm until the butter has melted.

STEP 3. Rinse the Party wings with a mixture of white vinegar and water. Pat dry. Fry the bare chicken wings for 8-10 minutes or until they have thoroughly cooked, the wings should be crisp and golden-brown.

STEP 4. Drain any excess oil using the wire rack. Inspect the inside of each chicken wing for any sign of undercooked meat. If it has cooked through, move on to the next step.

STEP 5. Toss the wings in the desired amount of buffalo sauce. Once the wings are evenly coated, serve and enjoy!

WHENEVER SOMEONE ASKS WHAT MY PASSION IS, I SAY FASHION IS MY FIRST LOVE, BUT COOKING IS WHERE MY HEART IS.

DYNAMITE SHRIMP

FOR THE SWEET CHILI SAUCE

- 1 teaspoon Mayonnaise
- 2 tablespoons Sweet Chili Sauce
- 1 tablespoon Sriracha sauce
- 1 dash Lemon Juice
- ½ tablespoon Soy Sauce

FOR THE SHRIMP

- 1 ½ pounds Jumbo Shrimp
- 4-6 cups Vegetable Oil
- ½ tablespoon Old Bay
- ¼ teaspoon Black Pepper
- ½ teaspoon Garlic Salt
- 1 Egg
- 2-3 cups Buttermilk
- ½ cup Cornstarch
- 1 cup Flour
- 1 tablespoon Cilantro, chopped

TOTAL TIME 15 MINUTES

SERVES 4

FOR THE SWEET CHILI SAUCE

STEP 1. In a mixing bowl, add mayonnaise, sweet chili sauce, Sriracha sauce, dash of lemon juice, and soy sauce. Thoroughly whisk together the ingredients to create the sweet chili sauce then set it aside.

FOR THE SHRIMP

STEP 2. Preheat the vegetable oil in the frying pan or deep fryer to 350ºF. Peel and devein the shrimp, then rinse with a mixture of white vinegar and water.

STEP 3. In a large mixing bowl add in old bay, black pepper, garlic salt, the egg and buttermilk to the shrimp. Mix well until shrimp is well coated.

STEP 4. In a separate mixing bowl, mix the cornstarch and flour together with a fork.

STEP 5. Dip the shrimp in the cornstarch-flour mixture. Drop the shrimp into the hot vegetable oil. Fry until crisp and golden brown, 5-6 minutes.

STEP 6. Place the shrimp on a wire rack to drain any excess oil. Coat the fried shrimp in sweet chili sauce then garnish with cilantro. Serve Immediately.

TURKEY SLIDERS

- 1-pound Ground Turkey
- 1 Egg
- ½ cup Panko Breadcrumbs
- ½ tablespoon Minced Garlic
- ½ teaspoon Black Pepper
- ½ teaspoon of Mrs. Dash
- ½ tablespoon Cajun seasoning
- ½ teaspoon of Onion Powder
- ¼ cup Chopped Onions
- ½ tablespoon Worcestershire
- 1 pack Hawaiian Roll Sliders
- Shredded Cheddar Cheese, to preference
- Olive Oil, to coat the pan
- ¼ cup White Onions, sautéed

TOTAL TIME 20 MINUTES
SERVES 4-5 (8-10 SLIDERS)

STEP 1. Add the ground turkey to a mixing bowl. Crack the egg into the bowl then pour in the breadcrumbs. Use clean hands to mix the egg and breadcrumbs into the turkey. It may take a few minutes to get it all thoroughly mixed in. Season with minced garlic, black pepper, Mrs. Dash, Cajun seasoning, and Onion Powder.

STEP 2. Shape the patties by hand. They should be about 3 inches in diameter and not too thick.

STEP 3. Sauté the chopped white onions in olive oil for 1-2 minutes in a skillet over medium-high heat, remove and set aside in a small bowl.

STEP 4. Turn the heat down to medium. Place the turkey sliders in the skillet; cook until well done, approximately 7-8 minutes on each side.

STEP 5. Top the sliders with a generous pinch of cheese. Cover the pan with a lid and reduce the heat to low for 1-2 minutes or until the cheese has melted. Place the sautéed onions on top of the melted cheese.

STEP 6. Cut the Hawaiian Rolls in half, so you have a top and bottom bun. Drizzle olive oil in the skillet and lightly toast both sides of the Hawaiian rolls. Place a turkey slider between the top and bottom bun, then serve.

CHEESESTEAK FRIES

- 4-6 cups Vegetable Oil (enough to fully cover the fries)
- 10-ounce Pre-Cut Fries
- 1 tablespoon Olive Oil
- 1 White Onion, chopped
- 1 Green Bell Pepper chopped
- 2-pounds Steak Umm Sliced Steak or Shredded Roast Beef
- ½ teaspoon Seasoned Salt
- Pinch of Black Pepper
- ⅛ teaspoon Garlic Salt
- ½ teaspoon Garlic Powder
- ½ teaspoon Onion Powder
- 1 cup Shredded Mozzarella Cheese
- 1 cup Shredded Parmesan Cheese

TOTAL TIME 15 MINUTES
SERVES 4

STEP 1. Preheat the vegetable oil in the deep fryer or frying pan to 350ºF. Drop in the fries. Cook to golden and crispy. Remove and drain the excess oil on a wire rack. Preheat the oven to 400ºF.

STEP 2. Add one tablespoon of olive oil to a sauté pan. Warm the pan over low heat. Sauté the onions and bell peppers for 1-2 minutes.

STEP 3. Add the sliced steak, use a metal spatula to break the steak into smaller chunks. Season the steak with seasoned salt, black pepper, garlic salt, garlic powder, and onion powder. Sauté for 10 minutes or until steak is cooked through.

STEP 4. Place the fries in a cast iron skillet then top with the steak. Sprinkle on the shredded cheese then bake in the preheated oven for 5-8 minutes or until the cheese has melted. Garnish with parsley and serve as a shareable appetizer.

Vegan
VIBES

VEGAN MAC & CHEESE

FOR THE CHEESE SAUCE

- 2 cups of Russet Potatoes, peeled and diced
- 1 cup of Carrots, peeled and diced
- 1-2 tablespoons Coconut Milk (optional, add to the cheese sauce while it warms)
- 1 tablespoon Cornstarch
- ½ cup Nutritional Yeast
- ½ cup Water
- ⅓ cup Olive Oil
- 1 tablespoon Lemon Juice

FOR THE MACARONI

- 1-pound box of Macaroni Elbows
- 1 teaspoon Salt
- ½ teaspoon Onion Powder
- ½ teaspoon Garlic Powder
- ½ teaspoon Smoked Paprika
- Vegan Parmesan Cheese, shredded

TOTAL TIME 45 MINUTES

SERVES 6

FOR THE CHEESE SAUCE

STEP 1. Boil the vegetables in a small pot of water for 15-20 or until softened.

STEP 2. Place boiled vegetables into a blender along with the coconut milk, cornstarch, nutritional yeast, water, olive oil, and lemon juice. Process the ingredients on high until smooth. Pour the sauce into a pot over medium heat. Simmer and stir until the sauce is creamy, about 5 minutes.

STEP 3. Preheat the oven to 350ºF. Meanwhile, bring water to a boil in a small or medium-sized pot, then pour in the elbows. Cook to al dente or somewhat firm.

STEP 4. Drain the macaroni elbows in a strainer. Pour the macaroni into a baking pan along with the cheese sauce. Season with salt, onion powder, garlic powder, and smoked paprika then stir well to complete coat the noodles in the cheese sauce and seasonings. Sprinkle in vegan mozzarella cheese and stir once more.

STEP 5. Place the vegan mac and cheese into the oven to bake for 30-35 minutes. Serve hot. Use a large spoon to serve.

FULLY LOADED SWEET POTATO

FOR THE SWEET POTATOES

STEP 1. Preheat the oven to 350ºF. Slice the potatoes in half then rub grapeseed oil over them. Season the inside of each potato with black pepper, cumin, garlic powder, salt, and chipotle seasoning.

STEP 2. Arrange the sweet potatoes on a baking sheet lined with parchment paper. Place the sweet potatoes in the oven to bake until they have softened, about 30 minutes.

FOR THE QUINOA

STEP 3. Pour the water, a pinch of salt, and quinoa into a small pot. Simmer the quinoa over medium heat until the water evaporates, 15-20 minutes. Fluff gently with a fork.

FOR THE SALSA

STEP 4. Combine the sliced grape tomatoes with the corn and black beans in a skillet. Season with black pepper, salt, crushed red pepper, and lime juice. Cook for 5-7 minutes. This will be the salsa.

STEP 5. Place the sweet potatoes on a serving plate then spread boysenberry jam over top. Place the quinoa and salsa over each potato. Serve.

FOR THE SWEET POTATOES

- 3 Sweet Potatoes
- Grape Seed Oil, to coat the potatoes
- ¼ teaspoon Black Pepper
- ¼ teaspoon Cumin
- ¼ teaspoon Garlic Powder
- ¼ teaspoon Himalayan Pink Salt
- ¼ teaspoon Chipotle Seasoning
- Boysenberry Jam, to taste

FOR THE QUINOA

- 2 cups Water
- Pinch Sea Salt
- 1 cup Quinoa

FOR THE SALSA

- 1 cup Grape Tomatoes, sliced
- 1 (15 ounce) can Corn, drained
- 1 (15 ounce) can Black Beans, drained
- Black Pepper, to taste
- Sea Salt, to taste
- ¼ teaspoon Crushed Red Pepper
- 1 Lime, squeezed

TOTAL TIME 30 MINUTES

SERVES 3-4

CURRY FRIED EGG ROLLS

- 4-6 cups Vegetable Oil
- ¼ cup Grape Seed Oil
- 1-pound bag Shredded Coleslaw
- ½ teaspoon Ground Ginger
- 1 tablespoon Curry Powder
- ½ teaspoon Minced Garlic
- ½ teaspoon Himalayan pink salt
- ½ teaspoon Tomato Paste
- Sriracha Sauce, to taste
- 1 teaspoon Soy Sauce
- 1 teaspoon Honey
- ¼ cup Water
- 2 tablespoons Cornstarch
- 6 Egg Roll Sheets

TOTAL TIME 30 MINUTES

SERVES 6

STEP 1. Preheat the vegetable oil to 350ºF in a frying pan or deep fryer. In a wok, warm the grapeseed oil over medium-high heat. Stir-fry the shredded coleslaw for 2-3 minutes or until al dente.

STEP 2. Season the coleslaw with ground ginger, curry powder, minced garlic, Himalayan pink salt, tomato paste, Sriracha sauce, and soy sauce. Continue to sauté for 5-7 minutes or until the shredded coleslaw has cooked down by half. Drizzle in the honey and mix into the coleslaw. Turn off the heat.

STEP 3. Mix the cornstarch and water in a bowl to create the wash. Lay the egg roll sheets out on a flat surface in a diamond shape. Use a brush to apply the wash to the edges of each sheet. Place an even amount of shredded coleslaw onto each egg roll sheet, being careful not to overfill. Create the egg roll by folding the sides over the coleslaw. Then, fold the bottom corner over the two folded sides and roll. Seal the egg rolls with the wash.

STEP 4. Drop the egg rolls in the fryer, cook until golden brown. Drain on a wire rack before serving.

VEGAN SPAGHETTI

- Grape Seed Oil, to coat the pan
- 4 Beyond Meat Sausage Links, sliced
- 5 Sliced Mushrooms
- 1 Red Bell Pepper
- 1 Green Bell Pepper
- 1 Yellow Bell Pepper
- 1 Orange Bell Pepper
- 3 Green Onions
- ½ cup White Onions
- 1 teaspoon Minced Garlic
- ½ teaspoon Oregano
- 1 teaspoon Cumin
- ½ teaspoon Crushed Red Peppers
- ¼ teaspoon Ginger Powder
- pinch of Black Pepper
- 12-ounces Veggie Spaghetti Noodles
- 1 medium can Tomato Sauce
- 1 tablespoon Tomato Paste

TOTAL TIME 45 MINUTES

SERVES 6-8

STEP 1. Warm the grape seed oil in a sauté pan over medium heat. Sauté the Beyond sausage for 5-7 minutes, set the sausage aside then drain the oil from the sauté pan.

STEP 2. Slice the mushrooms, slice the bell peppers into strips; and dice the green onions and white onions. Toss the veggies into a wok over high heat, sauté for 1-2 minutes.

STEP 3. Add the minced garlic, oregano, cumin, crushed red peppers, ginger powder, and black pepper into the wok. Continue to sauté the vegetables until they have softened.

STEP 4. Bring a pot of water to boil. Pour in the veggie spaghetti noodles and cook to al dente. Drain the noodles in a strainer.

STEP 5. Pour the tomato sauce and tomato paste into a pot over medium heat then add the sausage and peppers. Warm the tomato sauce to a low simmer. Stir and turn off the heat.

STEP 6. To serve, place the veggie spaghetti noodles onto a serving plate then pour the vegan meat sauce over top.

BLACK BEAN BURGERS

- Grape Seed Oil, to coat the pan
- ½ of a White Onion, chopped
- Half of a Green Bell Pepper, cut into 2-inch pieces
- 1 (14-ounce) can Black Beans, drained
- 1 (14-ounce) can Garbanzo Beans
- 3 Garlic Cloves, minced
- 1 Flax Egg (1 tablespoon Flax Meal mixed with 3 tablespoons water)
- ½ cup Breadcrumbs
- ¼ cup Flour
- 1 tablespoon Chili Powder
- ½ teaspoon Garlic Powder
- ¼ teaspoon Black Pepper
- 1 ½ teaspoons Cumin
- 1 teaspoon Cajun Seasoning
- 1 tbsp Olive Oil
- 2 tablespoons Barbecue Sauce
- 6 Burger Buns

TOTAL TIME 40 MINUTES

SERVES 6

STEP 1. Preheat the oven to 375ºF. In a sauté pan, cook the onions and peppers in grapeseed oil, over medium heat, until softened.

STEP 2. Line a baking sheet with parchment paper. Spread both the black and garbanzo beans out across the baking sheet. Place in the oven for 15 minutes to dry out the beans.

STEP 3. To a blender or food processor add the beans, onions, peppers, three garlic cloves, and one flax egg. Pulse until fully combined.

STEP 4. Transfer the bean mixture to a large mixing bowl. Season with breadcrumbs, flour, chili powder, garlic powder, black pepper, cumin, and Cajun seasoning. Use a large spoon or clean hands to thoroughly combine the mixture. Pat out six burger patties.

STEP 5. Place the patties onto a baking sheet lined with parchment paper. Bake for 10 minutes, flip the patties after 5 minutes.

STEP 6. Warm the olive oil in a grill pan. Grill the patties for 8 minutes on each side.

STEP 7. Serve the burgers with buns and your favorite burger toppings.

VEGAN CHEESESTEAK

FOR THE VEGGIES

- 3 cups + 2 tablespoons Grape Seed Oil, separated
- 1 Red Bell Peppers, medium sliced
- 1 Green Bell Peppers, medium sliced
- 1 Orange Bell Peppers, medium sliced
- ¾ cup White Onion, sliced

FOR THE BATTER

- ½ cup of Flour
- Pinch of Sriracha Sauce
- ¼ cup of Water
- 12-ounces Oyster Mushrooms
- 1 cup Panko Breadcrumbs

FOR THE CHEESE SAUCE

- ¼ cup Flour
- 2 tablespoons Water
- ¼ cup of Coconut Milk
- 3 slices of Vegan Provolone Cheese, broken into small pieces
- ¼ teaspoon Crushed Red Chili Peppers
- ¼ teaspoon Black Pepper
- 1 teaspoon Sriracha Sauce
- 2-3 Hoagie Rolls

TOTAL TIME 15 MINUTES

SERVES 2-3

FOR THE VEGGIES

STEP 1. Preheat 3 cups grapeseed oil to 350ºF in the frying pan or deep fryer. In a sauté pan, warm 2 tablespoons of grapeseed oil over medium heat. Add the peppers and onion to the sauté pan and cook to al dente. Set the peppers and onions aside.

FOR THE BATTER

STEP 2. In a mixing bowl, add flour, Sriracha sauce, and water. Mix the ingredients into a batter.

STEP 3. Dip the oyster mushrooms into the batter, tap off the excess then coat with panko crumbs.

STEP 4. Fry the oyster mushrooms to golden brown. Drain any excess oil from the mushrooms using a strainer. Drain on a wire rack.

FOR THE CHEESE SAUCE

STEP 5. In a saucepan, add flour, water, coconut milk, vegan provolone cheese, crushed red chili peppers, black pepper, and Sriracha sauce. Simmer the mixture for 10-15 minutes until thickened into a sauce. Stir occasionally.

STEP 6. To serve, toss the peppers and onions with the oyster mushrooms in a mixing bowl. Pour in the cheese sauce and toss once more. Fill a hoagie roll with the mushroom mixture then serve.

VEGAN MEATLOAF

FOR THE MEATLOAF

- 1 (16-ounce) can Chickpeas, drained
- 1 (16-ounce) can Kidney Beans, drained
- 1 cup Ground Flaxseed
- 1 cup Nutritional Yeast
- ½ cup Tahini
- ¼ cup Soy Sauce
- ¼ cup Unsweetened Almond Milk
- 2 teaspoon Onion Powder
- 2 teaspoon Garlic Powder
- ¼ teaspoon Ground Black Pepper

FOR THE GLAZE

- ½ cup Ketchup
- 2 tablespoon Brown Sugar
- 1 teaspoon Onion Powder
- 1 teaspoon Garlic Powder
- ½ teaspoon Paprika

TOTAL TIME 1 HOUR

SERVES 10

FOR THE MEATLOAF

STEP 1. Preheat the oven to 350ºF. Add the chickpeas and beans to a mixing bowl and mash them with a fork or a potato masher. Add the rest of the ingredients for the meatloaf and mix until well combined. You can also blend all the ingredients in a food processor.

STEP 2. Press mixture firmly into a parchment lined 9x5-inch loaf pan or similar. Feel free to place the mixture onto a lined baking sheet and form it into a loaf pan with your hands.

FOR THE GLAZE

STEP 3. To make the glaze, simply mix the ketchup, brown sugar, onion powder, garlic powder, and paprika in a mixing bowl until well combined.

STEP 4. Spread the glaze evenly over the top of the meatloaf then bake for 50 minutes.

STEP 5. Remove from the oven and cool for at least 5 minutes before slicing and serving.

COCONUT CURRY CHICKPEAS

STEP 1. Toast or "burn" the curry powder with a drizzle of grapeseed oil in a sauté pan. Burn for 1-2 minutes.

STEP 2. Toss in the carrots and bell peppers then sauté them in the curry powder to al dente.

STEP 3. Add the chickpeas, grape tomatoes, and tomato paste. While stirring, pour in the coconut milk. Lastly, season with oregano and cumin.

STEP 4. Simmer on low heat for about 15 minutes while stirring occasionally. Serve over rice.

- 1 tablespoon Grapeseed Oil
- 1 teaspoon Curry Powder
- 1 Carrot, diced
- 3 Bell Peppers (Tri-Colored & sliced into thin strips)
- 1 can Chickpeas
- 10 Grape Tomatoes, sliced
- ½ teaspoon Tomato Paste
- 1 (13.5 ounce) can Coconut Milk
- ¼ teaspoon Oregano
- ¼ teaspoon of Cumin

TOTAL TIME 25 MINUTES
SERVES 4

I LOVE COOKING FOR THE SAME REASON THAT I LOVE FASHION — THE THRILL OF CREATING SOMETHING NEW.

Getting SUM'N SWEET

FRIED OREOS

- 4-6 cups Vegetable Oil
- Boxed Pancake Mix
- 1 pack of Oreos
- 4-6 cups Vegetable Oil
- Vanilla Ice Cream, for serving

TOTAL TIME 20 MINUTES

SERVES 8-12

STEP 1. Preheat vegetable oil in the frying pan or deep fryer to 350ºF.

STEP 2. Prepare the pancake batter per the instructions on the box. Make a large serving if you plan to fry the whole pack of Oreos.

STEP 3. Dip the Oreos into the pancake batter for a thick coating. Allow the excess batter to drip back into the bowl.

STEP 4. Drop the Oreos into the frying pan or deep fryer and cook until they are golden brown. Flip the Oreos halfway through. Ensure that the Oreos are fully submerged in the oil.

STEP 5. Remove the Oreos and allow them to cool for a few minutes before serving with a scoop of vanilla ice cream.

PEACH COBBLER

- 1-pint of Vanilla Ice Cream, for serving
- Nonstick Spray

FOR THE PEACHES

- 4 cans Peaches in Heavy Syrup
- ½ cup White Sugar
- ½ cup Brown Sugar
- 1 teaspoon Cinnamon
- ¼ teaspoon Nutmeg
- 1 tablespoon Butter, divided
- ½ tablespoon Butter, softened
- 1 teaspoon Vanilla Extract
- 1 tablespoon Fresh Lemon Juice
- 1 tablespoon Cornstarch
- 2 Pie Crusts (refrigerated)

FOR THE CRUMB TOPPING

- 4 tablespoons Unsalted Butter
- ½ cup All-Purpose Flour
- ½ cup Brown Sugar
- ⅛ cup White Sugar
- ½ tablespoon Butter, melted

TOTAL TIME 45 MINUTES

SERVES 6

FOR THE PEACHES

STEP 1. Preheat the oven to 350ºF. Pour the peaches from all four cans into a mixing bowl, only using the juice from three. Set the juice from the fourth can aside in a separate bowl.

STEP 2. Add the white sugar, brown sugar, cinnamon, nutmeg, butter, and vanilla extract. Mix until the peaches are thoroughly coated.

STEP 3. In a pan, over medium low heat, melt half a tablespoon of butter, and pour in the peaches. Simmer for 2-3 minutes. To thicken the peaches, add cornstarch to the leftover peach juice. Use a fork to whisk together well, then slowly stir the cornstarch slurry into the pan. Continue to cook for 2-3 more minutes. Remove from heat once done.

FOR THE CRUMB TOPPING

STEP 4. Place the butter, flour, and brown sugar into a pot over medium-low heat. Mix well, the consistency will be thick. Turn off the heat then set aside in a separate bowl. Cool for 5-10 minutes before adding the white sugar. Use a spoon to combine until the mixture is crumbly.

STEP 5. Spray a baking dish with nonstick cooking spray. Line the dish with pie crust then carefully pour the peaches into the baking dish. Be careful not to overfill.

STEP 6. Use the remaining pie crust to create a lattice top over the baking dish then brush melted butter over top. Sprinkle crumb topping over the lattice crust. Place the cobbler in the oven to bake for about 30-45 minutes.

STEP 7. Allow to cool for 20 minutes before serving with vanilla ice cream

BANANA PUDDING

- 2 (3.4 oz) Instant Vanilla Pudding
- 1 (14-ounce) can Condensed Milk
- 8-ounce pack Cream Cheese, softened
- 3 cups Milk
- 1 tsp Vanilla Extract
- 1 pack of Butter Cookies
- 1 pack of Vanilla Wafers
- 4-6 Bananas, sliced
- 1 (12-ounce) container Cool Whip

STEP 1. Combine instant pudding, condensed milk, cream cheese, milk, and vanilla extract in a bowl. Use a whisk to mix ingredients into the pudding.

STEP 2. Spread the butter cookies and vanilla wafers along the bottom of a large bowl. Add a layer of pudding, then cookies, then a layer of bananas. Repeat steps until the mixture is finished. Top off with whipped cream, then add a layer of cookies on top.

STEP 3. Place the Banana Pudding in the refrigerator to set for at least 2 hours before serving.

LEMON POUND CAKE

- Nonstick Spray

FOR THE CAKE

- 2 sticks Butter, softened
- 1 cup Sugar
- 4 eggs
- 2 teaspoons Vanilla Extract
- 1 ½ cups Flour
- 1 teaspoon Baking Powder
- ½ teaspoon Salt
- ¼ cup Lemon Juice

FOR THE GLAZE

- ⅓ cup Lemon Juice
- ⅓ cup of Sugar

TOTAL TIME 1 HOUR

SERVES 10

STEP 1. Preheat the oven to 350ºF. Use butter or nonstick spray to grease a pound cake mold. In a medium bowl, combine the flour, baking powder, and salt.

STEP 2. Using a mixer, cream the butter. Add the sugar and continue to cream the butter until the ingredients have combined. With the mixer still going, crack in the eggs, then add the vanilla.

STEP 3. Pour the flour, baking powder, and salt into the creamed butter and mix well. Once the dry ingredients have been thoroughly combined, pour in the lemon juice. Mix until perfectly smooth.

STEP 4. Pour the mix into the pound cake mold. Bake in the oven until the center rises, and a toothpick inserted through the center comes out mostly clean, approximately 65 to 75 minutes.

STEP 5. Meanwhile, stir together the glaze in a small bowl.

STEP 6. When the cake has finished baking, let it cool in the pan for 15 minutes (it will still be warm). Run a knife around the sides to loosen the cake. Set a wire rack on a sheet pan with sides (to catch the glaze) and turn the cake out onto the rack.

STEP 7. Spread icing all over the top and sides of the cake and allow it to soak in. Repeat until all of the glaze is used, including any glaze that has dripped onto the sheet pan. Let cool at room temperature or, wrapped in plastic wrap, in the refrigerator. Serve at room temperature.

SWEET POTATO PIE

- 1-pound Sweet Potatoes
- ½ cup Butter, softened
- 1 cup White Sugar
- ½ cup Milk
- 2 large Eggs
- ½ teaspoon Ground Nutmeg
- ½ teaspoon Ground Cinnamon
- 1 teaspoon Vanilla Extract
- 1 (9-inch) Unbaked Pie Crust

TOTAL TIME 2 HOURS

SERVES 8

STEP 1. Boil the sweet potatoes skin-on for 40- 50 minutes, or until softened. Run cold water over the sweet potato and remove the skin. Preheat the oven to 350ºF.

STEP 2. Break the sweet potato apart in a bowl. Add the butter and blend well with a mixer. Stir in the sugar, milk, eggs, nutmeg, cinnamon, and vanilla. Blend on medium speed until the mixture is smooth. Pour the sweet potato filling into an unbaked pie crust.

STEP 3. Bake for 55-60 minutes or until a knife inserted through the center comes out clean. Remove the pie from the oven, cool for 30 minutes. The pie will puff up like a soufflé first, and then it will sink as it completely cools off. Serve at room temperature.

BROWNIES

- 1 cup of Sugar
- ½ cup of Flour
- ⅓ cup of Coco Powder
- ¼ teaspoon Baking Powder
- ¼ teaspoon Salt
- 2 Eggs
- ½ cup of Butter, melted
- 1 teaspoon Vanilla Extract
- Semi-Sweet Chocolate Chips, (add to preference)
- 1 cup Walnuts (can substitute with any nut)
- Heath bits, (add to preference)
- Reese's bits, (add to preference)
- 8-inch cake pan

TOTAL TIME 45 MINUTES
SERVES 8

STEP 1. Preheat the oven to 350ºF. In a mixing bowl, combine all of the dry ingredients (sugar, flour, coco powder, baking powder, salt). Use a fork to mix the ingredients together.

STEP 2. In a separate mixing bowl, whisk together all of the wet ingredients (eggs, butter, and vanilla extract).

STEP 3. Pour the wet ingredients into the dry ingredients. Add the chocolate chips, nuts, Heath bits, and Reese's bits. Whip thoroughly with a mixer.

STEP 4. Pour the brownie batter into a baking pan. Place the pan into the oven and bake for 30 minutes. When a toothpick inserted through the center of the brownies comes out clean, they are ready to serve.

CHOCOLATE CHIP COOKIES

- 1 cup White Sugar
- 1 cup Light Brown Sugar
- 3 cups Flour
- 1 teaspoon Sea Salt
- 1 teaspoon of Baking Soda
- ½ teaspoon Baking Powder
- 2 Large Eggs
- 1 cup Salted Butter, softened
- 2 tsp Vanilla Extract
- 2 cups Chocolate Chips
- Nonstick Spray

PREP TIME 2-3 HOURS
BAKE TIME 10 MINUTES
SERVES 12

STEP 1. In a mixing bowl, combine all of the dry ingredients (white sugar, light brown sugar, flour, sea salt, baking soda, and baking powder). Use a fork to mix the ingredients together.

STEP 2. In a separate mixing bowl, whisk together all of the wet ingredients (eggs, butter, and vanilla extract).

STEP 3. Pour the wet ingredients into the dry ingredients. Toss in the chocolate chips. Use a mixer to whip the ingredients for just a few minutes or until a cookie dough forms. Set the cookie dough in the refrigerator for 2- 3 hours.

STEP 4. Preheat the oven to 375ºF. Remove the cookie dough from the refrigerator. Use your hands to roll the cookie dough into any size cookie balls. The size of the cookie balls depends on how large you want the cookies.

STEP 5. Grease a baking sheet with butter or nonstick spray, set the cookie dough onto the baking sheet evenly spaced apart. Place the cookies into the oven to bake for 8-10 minutes or until lightly golden. Remove cookies before they have entirely baked and are still soft. Allow the cookies to cool and harden for 2-3 minutes.

CARROT CAKE

STEP 1. Preheat the oven to 325ºF. Butter two 9-inch cake pans; line the bottoms with parchment paper. grease the paper with butter, then sprinkle a light coat of flour.

STEP 2. Spread the pecans on a baking sheet and toast for 8 minutes, until fragrant. Cool and finely chop the pecans.

FOR THE CAKE

STEP 3. In a large mixing bowl, whisk the flour, baking powder, baking soda, cinnamon, and salt. In a small bowl, whisk the oil, buttermilk, and vanilla. In another large bowl, using a mixer, whip the eggs and sugar at high speed until pale, 5 minutes. Pour in the wet ingredients and mix. Then, whisk in the dry ingredients just until moistened. Use a large spoon to stir in the carrots and pecans. Divide the batter between the pans and bake the cakes for 55-60 minutes, until golden brown. Let the cakes cool on a rack for 30 minutes, then unmold the cakes and let cool completely.

FOR THE GLAZE

STEP 4. In a large bowl, whip the butter and cream cheese for at least 5 minutes. Beat in the vanilla, then the powdered sugar. Increase the speed and whip until the glaze is light and fluffy or for 3-4 minutes.

STEP 5. Peel off the parchment paper and place one cake layer onto a plate. Spread roughly a cup of the glaze over the first layer. Place the second cake layer on top of the first one, right side up. Spread all of the glaze over the top and sides. Cool the cake in the refrigerator for about 1 hour. Slice and serve.

FOR THE CAKE

- 1 cup Pecans
- 2 cups Flour
- 2 teaspoons Baking Powder
- 2 teaspoons Baking Soda
- 1 teaspoon Cinnamon
- 1 teaspoon Salt
- 1 cup Vegetable Oil
- ½ cup Buttermilk
- 1 ½ teaspoons Vanilla Extract
- 4 large Eggs
- 2 cups Sugar
- 1-pound Carrots, peeled and coarsely shredded

FOR THE GLAZE

- 2 sticks Butter (unsalted), softened
- 2 packets (16 ounce) Cream Cheese, softened
- 1 tablespoon Vanilla Extract
- 2 cups Powdered Sugar

TOTAL TIME 3.5 HOURS SERVES 8

TRES LECHE CAKE

- 1 ½ cup Flour
- 1 teaspoon of Baking Powder, softened
- 1 ½ cup of Unsalted Butter
- 1 cup of White Sugar
- 5 Eggs
- ½ teaspoon Vanilla Extract
- 2 cups Milk
- Nonstick Spray

FOR THE TOPPING

- 1 (14-ounce) can Sweetened Condensed Milk
- 1 (12-ounce) can Evaporated Milk
- 1 ½ cups Heavy Whipping Cream
- ½ teaspoon Vanilla Extract
- 1 cup White Sugar

TOTAL TIME 40 MINUTES

SERVES 6

STEP 1. Preheat the oven to 375ºF. In a mixing bowl, combine baking powder, flour, unsalted butter, white sugar, eggs, vanilla extract, and milk. Use a mixer to whip the ingredients into a cake batter.

STEP 2. Grease the cake pan with nonstick spray. Pour the batter into the pan then place the pan into the oven to bake for about 20 minutes. Once a toothpick inserted through its center comes out clean it is done.

STEP 3. Remove the baking pan from the oven. Poke small holes all over the cake using a knife, fork, or toothpick.

STEP 4. Pour condensed milk, evaporated milk, heavy cream, and vanilla into a mixing bowl. Add the sugar, then thoroughly mix to create the topping.

STEP 5. Pour the topping over the cake a spoonful at a time. Refrigerate until the cake is cool.

OREO CHEESECAKE

STEP 1. Use a blender to crush several Oreos into fine bits until you have 5 cups of blended Oreos.

STEP 2. In a mixing bowl, mix the crushed Oreos with melted butter. This will be the crust for the cheesecake. Press the crust evenly into the base of a standard size cake pan (preferably glass).

STEP 3. Use a mixer to whip together the cream cheese, powdered sugar, white sugar, vanilla extract and heavy cream until smooth. Crumble up to ten Oreos into the mixture then stir them in. Pour the mixture onto the Oreo crust.

STEP 4. Place a few whole Oreo cookies on top of the cheesecake, then put it in the refrigerator to set. After it has chilled for 3-4 hours, slice and serve.

- Oreos (5 cups when blended)
- 5 tablespoons melted butter
- 2 (8-ounce) packages Cream Cheese
- ½ cup Powdered Sugar
- ½ cup White Sugar
- 2 teaspoons Vanilla Extract
- ¾ cup of Heavy Cream

TOTAL TIME 3-4 HOURS

SERVES 6-8

APPLE TURNOVER

FOR THE TURNOVERS

- 4 Green Apples, peeled & diced
- 1 Egg
- 1 tablespoon Water
- 2 tablespoons Butter
- ⅓ cup White Sugar
- ⅓ cup Brown Sugar
- ¼ teaspoon Nutmeg
- 1 teaspoon Ground Cinnamon
- ½ teaspoon Vanilla Extract
- 1 tablespoon Cornstarch
- 1 tablespoon Water
- 1 (17.25-ounce) package Frozen Puff Pastry Sheets, thawed

FOR THE GLAZE

- ½ cup Powdered Sugar
- ⅓ cup Heavy Whipping Cream

TOTAL TIME 1 HOUR SERVES 8

FOR THE TURNOVERS

STEP 1. Place the diced apples in water to keep them from browning. In a separate bowl, mix one egg and one tablespoon of water together. Set aside.

STEP 2. In a saucepan, melt 1 tablespoon of butter over medium-low heat. Drain the water from apples and place them in the skillet. Add white sugar, brown sugar, nutmeg, cinnamon and vanilla extract. Cook and stir for 2 minutes, then add another tablespoon of butter and cook for another 2-3 minutes. In a separate bowl, stir together cornstarch and water. Pour into the skillet and mix well. Cook for another minute, or until the sauce has thickened. Remove from heat.

STEP 3. Preheat the oven to 400°F. Spread flour over a flat surface before unfolding the puff pastry sheets. Smooth any cracks by pressing them back together with your fingers. Use a rolling pin to roll out the sheet corners. Cut pastry dough into 4 smaller squares. Brush the egg wash on the edges of the squares.

STEP 4. Spoon the apples onto the center of each square. Fold over from corner to corner into a triangle shape, and press edges together to seal. Dip a fork in flour, then press the edges across the perimeter of the pastries to seal the turnovers. Using a knife make 3 slits on top of the pastries. Brush the eggwash over the pastry and place the turnovers on a baking sheet, leaving about 1 inch between them. Place in the freezer for 10-15 minutes.

STEP 5. Bake the turnovers for 20 minutes or until the are fluffy and golden brown. Cool completely before glazing.

FOR THE GLAZE

STEP 6. To make the glaze, mix together the powdered sugar and heavy whipping cream until you have a creamy icing. Drizzle the glaze over the cooled apple turnovers.

BLUEBERRY LEMON MUFFINS

FOR THE MUFFINS

STEP 1. Preheat the oven to 375ºF. In a mixing bowl, the combine flour, baking powder, salt, and sugar. Mix well.

STEP 2. Crack the eggs into the mixing bowl. Add the butter then pour in buttermilk, vanilla extract, and lemon juice. Whip all the ingredients with a mixer.

STEP 3. Toss in the blueberries. Mix the blueberries with a spoon until evenly distributed throughout the batter.

STEP 4. Use nonstick spray to grease a muffin pan. Pour the batter into each muffin cup, slightly under full. Place into the oven to bake for 20-25 minutes. Once a toothpick inserted through the center of each muffin comes out clean, the muffins are ready.

FOR THE GLAZE

STEP 5. Meanwhile, combine the powdered sugar, butter, milk, and lemon juice in a small mixing bowl. Whisk the ingredients thoroughly to create the glaze.

STEP 6. Drizzle the glaze over the top of the muffins then serve.

FOR THE MUFFINS

- 2 cups Flour
- 2 teaspoons Baking Powder
- ½ teaspoon of Salt
- 1 ¼ cup Sugar
- 2 Large Eggs
- 1 stick of Butter, softened
- ½ cup of Buttermilk
- ½ teaspoon of Vanilla Extract
- ¼ cup Lemon Juice
- 2 cups Blueberries
- Nonstick Spray

FOR THE GLAZE

- 4 tablespoons Powdered Sugar
- 1 tablespoon Butter
- 1 tablespoon Milk
- 2 tablespoons Lemon Juice

TOTAL TIME 35-40

SERVES 6-8

UPSIDE DOWN APPLE CAKE

FOR THE APPLES

- 4 tablespoons Butter, unsalted
- ½ cup Light Brown Sugar
- Pinch of Salt
- 2 Golden Delicious Apples, peeled and sliced

FOR THE CAKE

- 1 ½ cups All-Purpose Flour
- 1 cup Sugar
- 1 ½ teaspoons Baking Powder
- 1 teaspoon Kosher Salt
- 2 large Eggs
- ½ cup Milk
- 1 teaspoon Vanilla Extract
- 1 ½ sticks Butter (unsalted), melted

FOR THE GLAZE

- ¼ cup powdered sugar
- 1 tablespoon milk

TOTAL TIME 2 HOURS SERVES 6-8

FOR THE APPLES

STEP 1. Preheat the oven to 350ºF and line the bottom of a 9-inch cake pan with parchment paper. In a large bowl, mix the butter with the brown sugar and salt. Spread the mixture evenly in the lined cake pan. Arrange the apples wedges in the pan in 2 circles.

FOR THE CAKE

STEP 2. In the same bowl, whisk the flour with the sugar, baking powder and salt. In a small bowl, whisk the eggs with the milk and vanilla. Add the mixture to the dry ingredients along with the melted butter and whisk until smooth. Scrape the batter over the apples and spread evenly. Bake the cake on the lower oven rack until golden, springy, and a toothpick inserted in the center comes out clean, about 1 hour and 15 minutes.

STEP 3. Transfer the pan to a rack and cool for 30 minutes. Move the tip of a knife around the inside rim of the pan. Center a serving plate over the cake; carefully place the cake on the plate by flipping it over and removing the pan. Peel off the parchment paper then let the cake cool completely.

FOR THE GLAZE

STEP 4. In a small bowl, stir the powdered sugar with the milk into a glaze. Drizzle the glaze over the cake. Cut the cake into wedges and serve.

BANANA NUT BREAD

- 1 cup Sugar
- 1 ¼ cups Flour
- ½ teaspoon Salt
- 1 teaspoon Baking Soda
- 3 Bananas
- 2 Eggs
- ½ teaspoon Vanilla Extract
- ½ cup Butter, unsalted
- ½ cup Walnuts, chopped
- Nonstick Spray

TOTAL TIME 1 HOUR

SERVES 4

STEP 1. Preheat the oven to 350ºF. In a mixing bowl, combine sugar, flour, salt, and baking soda.

STEP 2. Mash the bananas, then add them to the mixing bowl. Crack the eggs in, then add vanilla, and butter. Use a mixer to whip the ingredients until well combined. Stir in the chopped walnuts.

STEP 3. Grease a baking dish with nonstick spray. Pour the mixture into a small baking dish. Place it in the oven to bake for 50 minutes or until a toothpick inserted through the center comes out clean.

STEP 4. Remove the bread from the oven and cool for 10 minutes before slicing and serving.

THE KITCHEN IS A PLACE TO EXPERIENCE HAPPY VIBES, MAKE GREAT MEMORIES AND BOND WITH LOVED ONES.

Sip

AFTER DARK

BOUGIE TEA
COSMOPOLITAN

- 1 ½ shots of Citrus Vodka
- ¼ shot Simple Syrup
- 1 shot of Fresh Lime Juice
- 2 shots of Cranberry Juice

SERVES 1 DRINK

STEP 1. Pour the citrus vodka, simple syrup, lime juice, and cranberry juice into a cocktail shaker. Shake vigorously to mix thoroughly.

STEP 2. Strain the liquid into a cocktail glass. Serve over ice, if you prefer.

FEELING JUICY
DAIQUIRI

STEP 1. Chill 2 cocktail glasses in the freezer for up to an hour.

STEP 2. Pour the light rum, fresh lime juice, and cranberry juice into a blender. Add a small amount of ice.

STEP 3. Blend the ice until it is finely crushed. Pour in the chilled cocktail glasses, then serve with a twist of lime.

- 4 Shots of Light Rum
- 2 shots of Fresh Lime Juice
- 2 shots of Cranberry Juice
- Ice
- 1 lime Twist

SERVES 2 DRINKS

LEAVE HIM ON READ

DARK N' STORMY

- 1 ½ shots of Dark Rum
- 3 shots of Ginger Beer
- 1 lime Wedge
- Ice

SERVES 1 DRINK

STEP 1. First, pour the rum over ice in an old-fashion, rocks, or lowball glass. Next, add ginger beer.

STEP 2. Garnish with a lime wedge and serve.

SLUT ME OUT
EXTRA DIRTY MARTINI

STEP 1. Pour two shots of vodka, then two shots of olive brine into a mixing glass with ice. Gently stir.

STEP 2. Strain the liquid into a chilled cocktail glass. Dispose of the ice.

STEP 3. Skewer 3, 6-inch olives then place the skewer in the martini glass to garnish.

- 2 shots of Vodka
- 2 ½ shots of Olive Brine
- 3 Olives
- 6-inch Skewer
- Ice

SERVES 1 DRINK

NAUGHTY BY NATURE
MARGARITA

- 1 ½ shots of Blanco Tequila
- 1 shot of Lemon Juice
- ¾ shot of Lime Juice Salt for rim (optional)
- 1 Lime Wedge
- 3 dashes Agave Syrup
- Ice

SERVES 1 DRINK

STEP 1. Add the blanco tequila, lemon juice, and lime juice to an ice-filled cocktail shaker. Add a pinch of agave syrup before shaking for a sweeter taste.

STEP 2. Strain into a chilled margarita glass filled with ice. Wet the fingertips, pinch the salt then press around the rim of the glass.

STEP 3. Garnish with a lime wheel.

SHOOT YA SHOT
MOJITO

STEP 1. Muddle the lime wedges, mint and sugar in a glass until the sugar has dissolved or until well mixed with simple syrup.

STEP 2. Pour ginger beer and white rum into the glass. Stir to combine. Garnish with mint.

- 5 Lime Wedges
- 5 Fresh Mint Leaves
- 3 Mint Sprigs
- 2 teaspoons Sugar (can substitute 1/2 shot of simple syrup)
- 1 shot of Ginger Beer
- 2 shots of White Rum

SERVES 1 DRINK

SOPHISTIRATCHET

HENNESSY LEMONADE

- 5 splashes Ginger Beer
- 3 ½ shots Hennessy
- 5 shots of Lemonade
- ¼ shot Fresh Lime Juice
- Ice

SERVES 1 DRINK

STEP 1. Combine the ginger beer, Hennessy, lemonade, and lime juice into a cocktail shaker. Add ice and shake well.

STEP 2. Strain the liquid into a cocktail glass before serving.

DRUNK TEXT

TEQUILA & GINGER BEER

STEP 1. Pour the tequila, reposado, blanco, ginger ale, ginger beer, and lime juice into a cocktail shaker. Shake vigorously.

STEP 2. Pour a cocktail glass garnish with lime and serve.

- 2 shots Tequila
- 1 shot Reposado
- 1 shot of Blanco
- 2 shots Ginger Ale
- 2 shots of Ginger Beer
- ¼ shot Lime Juice

SERVES 1 DRINK

POPPIN' PINK

PINK PANTIES

- 2 scoops Vanilla Ice Cream
- 1 can of Frozen Pink Lemonade
- 5 fresh Strawberries
- 6 shots Vodka

SERVES 1 DRINK

STEP 1. Blend vanilla ice cream, pink lemonade, and strawberries to a purée.

STEP 2. Pour the vodka into a cocktail shaker then add the purée. Cover and shake vigorously.

STEP 3. Serve in a chilled cocktail glass.

BRUNCH ME, PLEASE
WATERMELON MIMOSA

STEP 1. In a pitcher, stir together the watermelon juice and champagne.

STEP 1. Serve in a chilled glass garnished with fresh watermelon.

- 1/2 cup of Fresh Watermelon Juice
- 1 bottle Champagne

SERVES 4 DRINKS

Index

A

B

C

KITCHEN ENVY
PIECE SILICONE KITCHEN COOKING UTENSILS

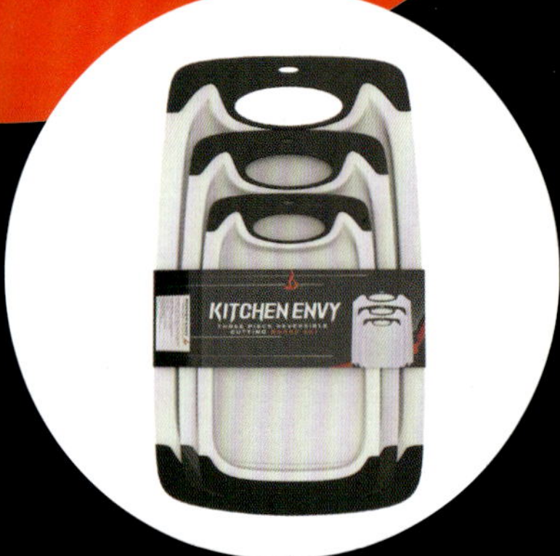

KITCHEN ENVY

KITCHEN ENVY

KITCHEN ENVY
AIR FRYER
DIGITAL CONTROL
KITCHEN ENVY
AIR FRYER
DIGITAL CONTROL

WHATS IN
THE BOX
KITCHEN ENVY
PIECE STAINLESS STEEL KNIFE SET
9 PCS
KITCHEN ENVY
KITCHEN ENVY
KITCHEN ENVY
PIECE SILICONE KITCHEN COOKING UNTENSILS *RED
10 PCS
KITCHEN ENVY
WARNING:
8 PIECE CLASSIC KITCHEN UTENSIL SET
8 PCS
KITCHEN ENVY
KITCHEN ENVY
PIECE STAINLESS STEEL KNIFE SET
9 PCS
KITCHEN ENVY
PIECE STAINLESS STEEL KNIFE SET
9 PCS
KITCHEN ENVY
PIECE STAINLESS STEEL KNIFE SET
9 PCS
KITCHEN ENVY
KITCHEN ENVY

Milk